MOJO FOR BEG

Your Fast Track To Next-Gen Programming

BENJAMIN SAMUEL

TABLE OF CONTENT

CHAPTER 10

PREFACE

Welcome to the exciting journey of learning Mojo, a revolutionary programming language poised to redefine how we approach performance-critical tasks without sacrificing the usability and accessibility that many developers have come to appreciate. In a world increasingly driven by data and the need for speed, Mojo emerges as a compelling solution, bridging the gap between the agility of dynamic languages and the raw power of systems-level programming.

This book is crafted for anyone eager to explore this new frontier – whether you're a seasoned Python developer seeking to unlock unprecedented performance gains, a curious programmer looking to expand your toolkit with a language designed for the modern computing landscape, or simply someone fascinated by the potential of next-generation programming paradigms.

Mojo is more than just another language; it's an ecosystem in the making, driven by the vision of making high-performance computing more approachable. It offers a unique blend of familiar syntax, inspired by Python, with powerful features like static typing, ownership concepts, and metaprogramming capabilities that unlock significant optimizations. This allows you to write code that can rival the speed of C++ while retaining a level of expressiveness and ease of development that feels remarkably intuitive.

Inside these pages, we will embark on a step-by-step exploration of Mojo, starting with the fundamental building blocks and gradually progressing towards more advanced concepts. We will delve into its unique features, understand how it achieves its performance prowess, and explore how you can leverage it to build efficient and robust applications.

As you navigate through the chapters, you'll not only learn the syntax and semantics of Mojo but also gain insights into the underlying principles that make it such a promising language for the future of programming. You'll discover how to structure your code effectively, manage resources efficiently, and harness the power of concurrency to tackle complex challenges.

The Mojo ecosystem is still in its early stages, full of potential and ripe for exploration. By learning Mojo now, you're not just acquiring a new skill; you're positioning yourself at the forefront of a technological evolution. This book aims to be your trusted guide as you embrace the dawn of high-performance programming with Mojo.

Let's begin this exciting adventure together!

CHAPTER 1

Welcome to the World of Mojo!

1.1 What Makes Mojo Special? Exploring its Power and Potential

Mojo's core appeal lies in its unique position as a language that aims to bridge the gap between the usability of dynamic languages like Python and the performance of static, systems-level languages such as C++ or Rust. This "best of both worlds" approach is a key differentiator.

One of the most significant aspects of Mojo is its performance focus. Unlike traditional scripting languages that often interpret code at runtime, leading to slower execution, Mojo is designed to be compiled. This compilation process allows the language to optimize the code for the underlying hardware, resulting in significantly faster execution speeds. This speed advantage is crucial for computationally intensive tasks, making Mojo particularly attractive for fields like AI, machine learning, and high-performance computing where processing large datasets and complex algorithms efficiently is paramount.

However, this performance doesn't come at the cost of developer experience. Mojo's syntax is intentionally designed to be very similar to Python. This familiarity means that developers already comfortable with Python can pick up Mojo relatively quickly, reducing the learning curve often associated with high-performance languages. You can expect to see familiar keywords and a similar code structure, making the transition smoother.

Furthermore, Mojo is being built with modern hardware architectures in mind. It's designed to effectively utilize features like parallelism (running tasks simultaneously on multiple processor cores) and vectorization (performing the same operation on multiple data points at once). This inherent awareness of hardware capabilities allows Mojo code to automatically leverage the power of modern CPUs and GPUs, leading to more efficient and faster computations without requiring developers to write complex, low-level code to manage these aspects manually.

Another crucial element of Mojo's potential is its planned interoperability with the Python ecosystem. Python boasts a vast and rich collection of libraries and tools used across various domains. Mojo aims to allow developers to seamlessly integrate Mojo code with existing Python projects. This means you could potentially write performance-critical parts of your application in Mojo to gain speed benefits while still leveraging the extensive Python library ecosystem for other functionalities. This gradual adoption path makes it easier for existing Python projects to benefit from Mojo's performance without requiring a complete rewrite.

In essence, Mojo strives to empower developers to write high-performance code with the ease and expressiveness they've come to expect from Python, opening up new possibilities for building demanding applications in areas like AI and scientific computing more efficiently.

1 2 Setting Up Your Mojo Environment: Installation and First Steps

Setting up your Mojo development environment is the crucial first step to writing and running Mojo code. As Mojo is a relatively new language, the installation process and available tools are still evolving, but here's a general guide based on the current methods:

Currently, the primary way to get started with Mojo is through the **Modular CLI (Command Line Interface)**. Modular is the company behind the Mojo programming language. The CLI provides the necessary tools to download the Mojo SDK (Software Development Kit), which includes the compiler, runtime, and other essential components.

Installation via the Modular CLI:

1.Install `modular`**:** The first step is to install the Modular CLI itself. This is typically done through a package manager or a direct script from Modular. The exact command might vary slightly depending on your operating system (macOS, Linux, Windows). You'll generally find the most up-to-date installation instructions on the official Modular website or their documentation. Look for a command that usually involves `curl` or `wget` to download and run an installation script.

2. For example, on macOS or Linux, it might look something like this (always refer to the official documentation for the exact command):

3. Bash

curl -O https://get.modular.com && chmod +x get.modular.com && ./get.modular.com
4.

5m This script will download and install the `modular` command-line tool on your system.

6. Authenticate with Modular: After installing the `modular` CLI, you'll likely need to authenticate with your Modular account. This step ensures you have access to the Mojo SDK. You'll probably be prompted to log in through your web browser when you run a command that requires authentication.

7. Install the Mojo SDK: Once the `modular` CLI is installed and you're authenticated, you can use it to download and install the Mojo SDK. The command for this is usually straightforward, like:

8. Bash

```
modular install mojo
```
9.

10. This command will download the necessary Mojo components to your system. The exact location where Mojo is installed will depend on your operating system and the Modular CLI's configuration.

Your First Steps: Creating and Running a Mojo Program:

1.Create a Mojo Source File: Open a plain text editor (like VS Code, Sublime Text, Notepad on Windows, or TextEdit on macOS). By convention, Mojo source files typically have the `.mojo` extension. Let's create a simple "Hello, Mojo!" program. Type the following code into your editor:

2. Code snippet

```
fn main():
    print("Hello, Mojo!")
```
3.

4. Save the File: Save this file with a name like `hello.mojo` in a directory of your choice.

5. Open Your Terminal or Command Prompt: Navigate to the directory where you saved the `hello.mojo` file using your terminal or command prompt.

6. Run the Mojo Program: To execute your Mojo code, you'll use the `mojo` command followed by the name of your source file:

7. Bash

mojo hello.mojo
8.

9. This command will compile (if necessary) and run your Mojo program. You should see the output:

Hello, Mojo!
10.

11. Integrated Development Environments (IDEs):

While you can write Mojo code in any text editor, using an Integrated Development Environment (IDE) can significantly enhance your development experience. Currently, support for Mojo in popular IDEs like VS Code is evolving. You might find extensions or plugins that provide features like syntax highlighting, code completion, and debugging support for Mojo. Keep an eye on the Modular documentation and community for updates on IDE support.

Important Considerations for Beginners:

Refer to Official Documentation: The installation process and available tools for Mojo are under active development. Always refer to the official Modular documentation (https://docs.modular.com/) for the most up-to-date and accurate instructions for your operating system.

Community Support: Engage with the Mojo community forums or discussion groups. Other beginners and experienced users can be valuable resources for troubleshooting installation issues and getting started.

Patience: As a new language, the tooling and ecosystem around Mojo are still growing. Be patient with the development process and expect updates and improvements over time.

By following these steps, you should be able to successfully set up your Mojo environment and run your first Mojo program. This foundational step will allow you to start exploring the exciting features and capabilities of the language.

1.3 Your First "Hello, Mojo!" Program: Understanding Basic Syntax

Let's break down the basic syntax of your first "Hello, Mojo!" program:

Code snippet

```
fn main():
    print("Hello, Mojo!")
```

This simple program introduces several fundamental concepts in Mojo syntax:

fn Keyword: Defining a Function
In Mojo, the keyword fn is used to define a function. Functions are blocks of reusable code that perform specific tasks. The basic structure of a function definition in Mojo looks like this:

Code snippet

```
fn function_name(parameter1: Type1, parameter2: Type2, ...) -> ReturnType:
    # Code to be executed within the function
    return some_value
```

In our "Hello, Mojo!" program, we have `fn main():`. This defines a function named `main`. The parentheses `()` indicate that this function doesn't take any input parameters. The absence of `->` `ReturnType` means that this function doesn't explicitly return a value (though in many programming environments, the `main` function might implicitly return an exit code).

main() Function: The Entry Point
The main function is special in many programming languages, including Mojo. It serves as the entry point of your program. When you run a Mojo program, the execution typically begins with the code inside the main function. Every standalone Mojo program

needs to have a main function.

Indentation: Defining Code Blocks

Notice that the line print("Hello, Mojo!") is indented under the fn main(): line. In Mojo (similar to Python), indentation is crucial. It's used to define code blocks. Statements that are part of the same block (like the code inside a function) must have the same level of indentation. Consistent use of indentation makes Mojo code readable and helps the compiler understand the structure of your program. Typically, four spaces are used for each level of indentation, though some editors might use tabs (it's generally recommended to stick to spaces for consistency).

print() Function: Outputting Information

print() is a built-in function in Mojo that allows you to display output to the console (your terminal or command prompt). In our example, print("Hello, Mojo!") will display the text "Hello, Mojo!" on the screen when the program is executed. The text enclosed in double quotes " is called a string literal.

String Literals:

"Hello, Mojo!" is a string literal. It represents a sequence of characters. In Mojo, you can use double quotes " to enclose strings.

In Summary:

The "Hello, Mojo!" program demonstrates the basic structure of a simple Mojo program:

1.You define a function using the fn keyword.

2. The `main` function acts as the starting point of your program's execution.

3. Indentation is used to group statements into code blocks.

4. The `print()` function is used to display output.

5. Strings are enclosed in double quotes.

This seemingly simple program lays the foundation for understanding how to structure more complex Mojo code. As we move forward, you'll see these fundamental elements being used in various ways to build more sophisticated programs.

CHAPTER 2

The Building Blocks: Variables and Data Types

2.1 Understanding Variables: Storing and Managing Information

Variables are fundamental to programming. They are like named containers in your computer's memory that you can use to store and manage different kinds of information (data). In Mojo, you use variables to hold values that your program can then access and manipulate.

Here's a breakdown of understanding variables in Mojo:

Declaration and Initialization: Before you can use a variable, you typically need to declare it and often initialize it with an initial value. Mojo offers flexibility in how you declare variables, sometimes allowing type inference.

Explicit Type Declaration: You can explicitly specify the data type of a variable during declaration using the `var` keyword followed by the variable name, a colon, and the type.

Code snippet

```
var age: Int = 30
var name: String = "Alice"
var is_student: Bool = false
var height: Float = 1.75
```

In these examples:

age is declared as an `Int` (integer) and initialized to `30`.

name is declared as a `String` (text) and initialized to `"Alice"`.

is_student is declared as a `Bool` (boolean, representing true or false) and initialized to `false`.

height is declared as a `Float` (floating-point number) and initialized to `1.75`.

Type Inference (Often Preferred): Mojo often allows you to omit the explicit type declaration, and the compiler can infer the type based on the initial value assigned to the variable. This can make your code more concise.

Code snippet

var count = 0 # Mojo infers 'count' to be an Int

```
var message = "Hello" # Mojo infers 'message' to be a String
var pi = 3.14159 # Mojo infers 'pi' to be a Float
var active = true # Mojo infers 'active' to be a Bool
```

Variable Naming Rules: When you name your variables, there are certain rules you need to follow:

Variable names must start with a letter (a-z, A-Z) or an underscore (_).

Subsequent characters can be letters, numbers (0-9), or underscores.

Variable names are case-sensitive (myVariable is different from myvariable).

You cannot use Mojo keywords (like fn, var, if, etc.) as variable names.

It's a good practice to choose descriptive names that indicate the purpose of the variable (e.g., userAge instead of a).

Assigning and Reassigning Values: Once a variable is declared, you can assign a value to it using the assignment operator (=). If the variable is declared with `var` (meaning it's mutable), you can also reassign it to a different value (of the same or a compatible type, depending on Mojo's type system rules).

Code snippet

```
var score: Int = 100
print(score)  # Output: 100

score = 120  # Reassigning a new value to 'score'
print(score)  # Output: 120

var greeting = "Hi"
print(greeting) # Output: Hi

greeting = "Hello" # Reassigning 'greeting'
print(greeting) # Output: Hello
```

Constants (Immutable Variables): In addition to `var`, Mojo might also have a way to declare constants – variables whose values cannot be changed after their initial assignment. This is often done using a keyword like `let` in some languages. While the exact syntax for constants in Mojo might evolve, the concept is important for storing values that should remain fixed throughout the program's execution (e.g., the value of pi).

Code snippet

```
# Example of a constant (syntax might be slightly different in final
Mojo version)
let PI: Float = 3.14159
# PI = 3.14  # This would likely result in an error
```

Scope of Variables: The scope of a variable refers to the region of your code where the variable is accessible. Variables declared inside a function, for example, are typically only accessible within that function. We'll delve deeper into scope when we discuss functions.

Understanding how to declare, name, assign, and manage variables is a fundamental building block for writing any program. They allow you to store and work with data dynamically as your program executes.

2.2 Exploring Fundamental Data Types: Integers, Floats, and Booleans

Data types are classifications that specify the kind of values a variable can hold and the types of operations that can be performed on them. Mojo, like most programming languages, has fundamental data types that serve as the basic building blocks for representing different kinds of information. Let's explore three essential ones: **Integers**, **Floats**, and **Booleans**.

1. Integers (Int)

Integers are whole numbers; they do not have a fractional or decimal part. They can be positive, negative, or zero. Examples of integers include -5, 0, 10, 1000.

In Mojo, the primary keyword for representing integers is often `Int`. You might also encounter variations like `Int8`, `Int16`, `Int32`, `Int64`, which specify the number of bits used to store the integer, thus defining the range of values it can hold. For beginners, `Int` often defaults to a reasonable size (like 32 or 64 bits) for general use.

Code snippet

```
var whole_number: Int = 10
var negative_number: Int = -5
var zero: Int = 0

print(whole_number)    # Output: 10
print(negative_number) # Output: -5
print(zero)         # Output: 0
```

Operations on Integers: Common mathematical operations can be performed on integers, such as:

Addition: + (e.g., 5 + 3 results in 8)

Subtraction: - (e.g., 10 - 4 results in 6)

Multiplication: * (e.g., 2 * 6 results in 12)

Division (Integer Division): / (e.g., 7 / 3 might result in 2 in some contexts, discarding the remainder. Be aware of potential behavior and related operators for floating-point division)

Modulo (Remainder): % (e.g., 7 % 3 results in 1)

Code snippet

```
var a: Int = 15
var b: Int = 4

print(a + b)   # Output: 19
print(a - b)   # Output: 11
print(a * b)   # Output: 60
print(a / b)   # Output: (Potentially 3, depending on Mojo's integer division behavior)
print(a % b)   # Output: 3
```

2. Floating-Point Numbers (Float)

Floating-point numbers are used to represent numbers that have a fractional part or decimal places. Examples include 3.14, -0.5, 2.0, 1.618.

In Mojo, the keyword for representing single-precision floating-point numbers is often Float32, and for double-precision, it's Float64 (which is commonly referred to as just Float in many contexts for general use). Double-precision floats offer more accuracy.

Code snippet

```
var pi_value: Float64 = 3.14159
var half: Float32 = 0.5
var temperature: Float = 25.5 # Assuming 'Float' defaults to Float64

print(pi_value)   # Output: 3.14159
print(half)       # Output: 0.5
print(temperature) # Output: 25.5
```

Operations on Floats: Similar mathematical operations can be performed on floats:

Addition: + (e.g., 1.5 + 2.7 results in 4.2)

Subtraction: - (e.g., 5.0 - 1.2 results in 3.8)

Multiplication: * (e.g., 3.0 * 2.5 results in 7.5)

Division (Floating-Point Division): / (e.g., 7.0 / 3.0 results in approximately 2.333...)

Code snippet

```
var x: Float = 2.0
var y: Float = 3.5

print(x + y)   # Output: 5.5
print(y - x)   # Output: 1.5
print(x * y)   # Output: 7.0
print(y / x)   # Output: 1.75
```

3. Booleans (`Bool`)

Booleans represent truth values. They can have only two possible states: `true` or `false`. Booleans are fundamental for decision-making and controlling the flow of execution in programs.

In Mojo, the keyword for the boolean data type is likely `Bool`.

Code snippet

```
var is_valid: Bool = true
var has_finished: Bool = false

print(is_valid)     # Output: true
print(has_finished) # Output: false
```

Operations on Booleans (Logical Operators): Common logical operations are performed on boolean values:

AND: and (or && in some languages, check Mojo's syntax). Results in true only if both operands are true.

OR: or (or | |). Results in true if at least one of the operands is true.

NOT: not (or !). Inverts the boolean value (if it's true, it becomes false, and vice versa).

Code snippet

```
var p: Bool = true
var q: Bool = false

print(p and q)   # Output: false
print(p or q)    # Output: true
print(not p)     # Output: false
print(not q)     # Output: true
```

Understanding these fundamental data types is crucial because they form the basis for representing all kinds of data in your programs. When you declare a variable, you're essentially telling the computer what kind of information you intend to store in that memory location, which in turn dictates how that information can be manipulated.

2.3 Working with Strings: Text Manipulation in Mojo

Strings are used to represent sequences of characters, essentially text. In Mojo, you'll use strings to handle words, sentences, paragraphs, or any other textual data. Here's an overview of working with strings in Mojo:

Creating Strings: You typically create string literals by enclosing text within double quotes (").

Code snippet

```
var message: String = "Hello, Mojo!"
var name: String = "Alice"
var empty_string: String = ""
```

Basic String Operations:

Concatenation: You can combine two or more strings together to create a new string. The operator for concatenation in Mojo is likely to be + (similar to Python).

Code snippet

```
var greeting: String = "Hello"
var recipient: String = "World"
var full_greeting: String = greeting + ", " + recipient + "!"
print(full_greeting)  # Output: Hello, World!
```

String Length: You'll often need to know the number of characters in a string. Most languages provide a way to get the length of a string, perhaps using a function like `len()` or a property of the string object. Check Mojo's documentation for the specific method.

Code snippet

```
var text: String = "Mojo Programming"
# Assuming 'len()' function exists (check Mojo docs)
# var length: Int = len(text)
# print(length) # Output: 16
```

Accessing Characters (Indexing): Strings are often treated as sequences, meaning you can access individual characters within them using an index. Indices typically start from 0 for the first character.

Code snippet

```
var language: String = "Mojo"
# Assuming indexing works like Python (check Mojo docs)
# var first_char: String = language[0]
# var second_char: String = language[1]
# print(first_char)  # Output: M
# print(second_char) # Output: o
```

String Slicing: You can extract a portion (substring) of a string by specifying a range of indices.

Code snippet

```
var phrase: String = "Learning Mojo is fun!"
# Assuming slicing works like Python (check Mojo docs)
# var substring1: String = phrase[0:8]   # Characters from index 0
up to (but not including) 8
```

```
# var substring2: String = phrase[9:]    # Characters from index 9
to the end
# print(substring1) # Output: Learning
# print(substring2) # Output: Mojo is fun!
```

String Formatting (Interpolation): Often, you'll want to embed the values of variables directly within a string. This is known as string formatting or interpolation. Mojo's syntax for this might resemble Python's f-strings or other similar mechanisms.

Code snippet

```
var username: String = "coder123"
var score: Int = 95
# Assuming string interpolation syntax (check Mojo docs)
# print(f"User {username} achieved a score of {score}.")
# Or a similar syntax like:
# print("User \(username) achieved a score of \(score).")
```

String Methods: Strings often come with built-in methods that allow you to perform various operations, such as:

Changing case (e.g., converting to uppercase or lowercase).

Checking if a string starts or ends with a particular substring.

Finding the index of a substring.

Replacing parts of a string.

Splitting a string into a list of substrings based on a delimiter.

Removing leading or trailing whitespace.

You'll need to consult Mojo's standard library documentation to see the specific methods available for string manipulation. Examples might look something like this (syntax is illustrative and needs to be confirmed with Mojo's documentation):

Code snippet

```
var text_example: String = " Mojo is Awesome! "

# Assuming methods like these exist (check Mojo docs)
# var lower_case: String = text_example.lower()
# var upper_case: String = text_example.upper()
# var stripped: String = text_example.strip()
# var starts_with_mojo: Bool = text_example.startswith("Mojo")
# var replaced: String = text_example.replace("Awesome", "Powerful")

# print(lower_case)    # Output:  mojo is awesome!
# print(upper_case)    # Output:  MOJO IS AWESOME!
```

```
# print(stripped)       # Output: Mojo is Awesome!
# print(starts_with_mojo)  # Output: false (due to leading spaces)
# print(replaced)       # Output:   Mojo is Powerful!
```

Working with strings is a fundamental part of most programming tasks, from displaying messages to processing user input and handling textual data. As you learn Mojo, be sure to explore the available string manipulation features in its standard library.

CHAPTER 3

Controlling the Flow: Logic and Decisions

3.1 Making Choices with if, elif, and else Statements

Conditional statements, often using `if`, `elif` (short for "else if"), and `else`, are essential for creating programs that can make decisions and execute different blocks of code based on whether certain conditions are true or false. Let's explore how these work in Mojo:

The `if` Statement: The `if` statement is used to execute a block of code only if a specified condition is true. The basic syntax looks like this:

Code snippet

```
if condition:
    # Code to be executed if the condition is true
```

The `condition` is an expression that evaluates to a boolean value (`true` or `false`). If the condition is `true`,[1] the indented block of code following the `if` statement is executed. If the condition is `false`,[2] that block of code is skipped.

Code snippet

```
var temperature: Int = 25

if temperature > 20:
    print("It's warm!")
```

In this example, the message "It's warm!" will be printed because the condition `temperature > 20` (25 > 20) is true.

The `else` Statement: The `else` statement provides a block of code that is executed if the condition in the preceding `if` statement is false. An `else` block is optional and can only come after an `if` block (and any `elif` blocks).

Code snippet

```
var temperature: Int = 15

if temperature > 20:
    print("It's warm!")
else:
    print("It's not warm.")
```

Here, the condition `temperature > 20` (15 > 20) is false, so the code inside the `else` block will be executed, and "It's not warm." will be printed.

The `elif` Statement: The `elif` (else if) statement allows you to check multiple conditions in sequence. It comes after an `if` statement and before an optional `else` statement.[3] If the `if` condition is false, each `elif` condition is checked in order. The block of code corresponding to the first true `elif` condition is executed, and the rest of the `elif` and the `else` blocks are skipped.

Code snippet

```
var score: Int = 75

if score >= 90:
    print("Grade: A")
elif score >= 80:
    print("Grade: B")
elif score >= 70:
    print("Grade: C")
elif score >= 60:
    print("Grade: D")
else:
    print("Grade: F")
```

In this case, the condition `score >= 70` (75 >= 70) is the first true condition encountered after the initial `if` condition is false. Therefore, "Grade: C" will be printed.

Chaining `if`, `elif`, **and** `else`: You can have multiple `elif` statements to check for various conditions. The flow of execution will go through each condition in order until one evaluates to `true`, at which point its corresponding code block is executed, and the rest of the conditional structure is skipped. If none of the `if` or `elif` conditions are true, and an `else` block is present, the code inside the `else` block will be executed.

Nested `if` **Statements:** You can also have `if` statements (and `elif`, `else`) nested within other `if` statements. This allows for more complex decision-making based on multiple levels of conditions. However, deeply nested `if` statements can sometimes make code harder to read, so it's often better to find more streamlined ways to express complex logic if possible.

Code snippet

```
var has_license: Bool = true
var age: Int = 18

if has_license:
   if age >= 17:
      print("Can drive.")
   else:
      print("Cannot drive due to age.")
else:
   print("Cannot drive without a license.")
```

In this example, the outer `if` checks if the person has a license, and if so, the inner `if` checks their age.

if, elif, and else statements provide the control flow necessary to make your programs dynamic and responsive to different inputs and situations. They are fundamental tools for implementing logic and decision-making in your Mojo code.

3. 2 Repeating Actions with for and while Loops

Loops are fundamental control flow structures that allow you to execute a block of code repeatedly. Mojo, like most programming languages, provides mechanisms for creating loops, primarily through for and while statements.

1. The for Loop:

The for loop is typically used to iterate over a sequence of items, such as elements in a list, characters in a string, or a range of numbers. The basic structure in Mojo might look similar to Python's for loop:

Code snippet

```
# Iterating over a sequence (e.g., a list)
var my_list = [1, 2, 3, 4, 5]
for item in my_list:
    print(item)

# Iterating over a range of numbers
# Assuming 'range()' function exists (check Mojo docs)
# for i in range(0, 5): # Iterates from 0 up to (but not including) 5
#     print(i)

# Iterating over characters in a string
var text = "Mojo"
for char in text:
    print(char)
```

Let's break down the common uses:

Iterating over a sequence: When you have a collection of items (like a list), the `for` loop allows you to process each item one by one. The loop variable (`item` in the first example) takes on the value of each element in the sequence during each iteration.

Iterating over a range: Often, you need to repeat an action a specific number of times. The `range()` function (or its Mojo equivalent) is commonly used to generate a sequence of numbers. You can specify the starting point, the ending point (exclusive), and an optional step value.

Iterating over characters in a string: Strings can also be treated as sequences of characters, allowing you to loop through each character individually.

2. The `while` Loop:

The `while` loop is used to repeatedly execute a block of code as long as a specified condition remains true. The basic syntax looks like this:

Code snippet

```
while condition:
    # Code to be executed as long as the condition is true
        # It's crucial to have something inside the loop that can
eventually make the condition false
    # to avoid an infinite loop.
```

The `condition` is evaluated before each iteration. If it's true, the code block inside the `while` loop is executed. This process continues until the condition becomes false, at which point the loop terminates, and the program[1] execution continues with the code following the loop.

Here's an example of using a `while` loop to count down:

Code snippet

```
var count = 5
while count > 0:
    print(count)
    count = count - 1

print("Blast off!")
```

In this example:

1. The variable `count` is initialized to 5.

2. The `while` loop continues as long as `count` is greater than 0.

3. Inside the loop, the current value of `count` is printed, and then `count` is decremented by 1.

4. Once `count` becomes 0, the condition `count > 0` is false, and the loop terminates.

5. Finally, "Blast off!" is printed.

Important Considerations for Loops:

Infinite Loops: With `while` loops, it's crucial to ensure that the condition will eventually become false. If the condition never becomes false, you'll create an infinite loop, and your program will run indefinitely (or until you manually stop it).

Loop Control Statements: Mojo might also include statements like `break` and `continue` to control the flow of execution within loops:

`break`: Immediately terminates the loop and transfers control to the statement following the loop.

`continue`: Skips the rest of the current iteration and proceeds to the next iteration of the loop.

Code snippet

```
# Example with 'break'
for i in range(0, 10):
    if i == 5:
        break
    print(i) # Output: 0 1 2 3 4

# Example with 'continue'
for i in range(0, 5):
    if i == 3:
        continue
    print(i) # Output: 0 1 2 4
```

Loops are powerful tools for automating repetitive tasks and processing collections of data. Understanding how to use `for` and `while` loops effectively is essential for writing more complex and efficient Mojo programs.

3.3 Controlling Loop Execution: break and continue

`break` and `continue` are control flow statements that provide you with more fine-grained control over the execution of loops (`for` and `while`). They allow you to alter the normal iteration behavior based on specific conditions within the loop.

1. The `break` Statement:

The `break` statement is used to immediately terminate the innermost loop (the loop it is directly enclosed within). When a `break` statement is encountered, the program's execution jumps to the statement immediately following the loop. Any remaining iterations of the loop are skipped.

Here's an example using a `for` loop and `break`:

Code snippet

```
# Assuming 'range()' exists in Mojo
for i in range(0, 10):
    if i == 5:
        print("Breaking out of the loop at i =", i)
        break
    print("Current value of i:", i)
print("Loop finished.")
```

Output of this code would be:

Current value of i: 0
Current value of i: 1
Current value of i: 2
Current value of i: 3
Current value of i: 4
Breaking out of the loop at i = 5
Loop finished.

In this example, the loop is intended to run from 0 to 9. However, when the value of i becomes 5, the condition i == 5 is true, the break statement is executed, and the loop terminates immediately. The message "Loop finished." is then printed.

Here's an example using a while loop and break:

Code snippet

```
var counter = 0
while counter < 10:
    print("Counter:", counter)
    counter = counter + 1
    if counter == 7:
        print("Breaking out of the while loop at counter =", counter)
        break
print("While loop ended.")
```

Output:

Counter: 0
Counter: 1
Counter: 2
Counter: 3

Counter: 4
Counter: 5
Counter: 6
Breaking out of the while loop at counter = 7
While loop ended.

The while loop continues as long as counter is less than 10. When counter reaches 7, the break statement is executed, and the loop terminates.

2. The continue Statement:

The continue statement is used to skip the rest of the code within the current iteration of a loop and proceed directly to the next iteration. The loop's condition is then re-evaluated (in the case of a while loop) or the next item in the sequence is processed (in the case of a for loop).

Here's an example using a for loop and continue:

Code snippet

```
# Assuming 'range()' exists in Mojo
for i in range(0, 5):
    if i == 2:
        print("Skipping iteration where i =", i)
        continue
    print("Current value of i:", i)
```

Output:

Current value of i: 0
Current value of i: 1
Skipping iteration where i = 2

Current value of i: 3
Current value of i: 4

When `i` is 2, the condition `i == 2` is true, the `continue` statement is executed, and the rest of the code within that iteration (the `print("Current value of i:", i)`) is skipped. The loop then proceeds to the next iteration where `i` is 3.

Here's an example using a `while` loop and `continue`:

Code snippet

```
var number - 0
while number < 5:
    number = number + 1
    if number == 3:
        print("Skipping number:", number)
        continue
    print("Processing number:", number)
```

Output:

```
Processing number: 1
Processing number: 2
Skipping number: 3
Processing number: 4
Processing number: 5
```

In this `while` loop, when `number` becomes 3, the `continue` statement is executed, causing the `print("Processing number:", number)` line to be skipped for that iteration. The loop then proceeds to the next iteration where `number` becomes 4.

Key Differences:

`break` terminates the entire loop.

`continue` terminates only the current iteration and proceeds to the next one.

Understanding and using `break` and `continue` effectively can make your loops more flexible and allow you to handle specific conditions within your iterative processes. They are powerful tools for controlling the flow of execution within loops.

CHAPTER 4

Organizing Your Code: Functions

4.1 Defining and Calling Your First Functions

Functions are fundamental building blocks in programming that allow you to encapsulate a block of code with a specific name. This allows you to reuse that code multiple times in your program without having to rewrite it each time. Functions can take input values (parameters) and can also return output values.

1. Defining a Function:

In Mojo, you define a function using the `fn` keyword, followed by the function name, a list of parameters (if any) with their types, an optional return type, and then the body of the function enclosed in an indented block.

The general syntax for defining a function in Mojo looks like this:

Code snippet

```
fn function_name(parameter1: Type1, parameter2: Type2, ...) ->
ReturnType:
    # Statements that make up the function's body
    # ...
    return value  # If the function has a return type
```

Let's break down each part:

`fn`: This keyword signifies the start of a function definition.

`function_name`: This is the identifier you'll use to call or invoke the function later in your code. Choose a descriptive name that indicates what the function does.

`(parameter1: Type1, parameter2: Type2, ...)`: This is the parameter list. Parameters are input values that the function can receive. Each parameter has a name and a specified type (e.g., `name: String`, `age: Int`). A function can have zero or more parameters. If there are no parameters, you simply have empty parentheses `()`.

`-> ReturnType`: This is optional and specifies the type of the value that the function will return. If a function doesn't return any value explicitly, this part might be omitted (or it might implicitly return a special type like `None` in some languages, check Mojo's conventions).

`::` A colon marks the end of the function signature (the part before the indented block).

`# Statements that make up the function's body`: This is the indented block of code that contains the instructions the function will execute when called.

`return value`: If the function is supposed to return a value (as indicated by `ReturnType`), the `return` statement is used to send that value back to the part of the code that called the function.

Example of a Simple Function:

Code snippet

fn greet(name: String):

```
print("Hello, \(name)!")
```

In this example:

fn indicates it's a function definition.

greet is the name of the function.

(name: String) defines a single parameter named name of type String.

There's no -> ReturnType, which means this function doesn't explicitly return a value; it performs an action (printing).

The indented line print("Hello, \(name)!") is the body of the function. It uses string interpolation (likely using \()) to insert the value of the name parameter into the greeting message.

Example of a Function that Returns a Value:

Code snippet

```
fn add(x: Int, y: Int) -> Int:
    let sum: Int = x + y
    return sum
```

In this example:

add is the function name.

(x: Int, y: Int) defines two parameters, x and y, both of type Int.

`-> Int` specifies that this function will return a value of type `Int`.

Inside the function, the sum of `x` and `y` is calculated and stored in a variable `sum`.

The `return sum` statement sends the value of `sum` back to where the function was called.

2. Calling (Invoking) a Function:

To execute the code inside a function, you need to call or invoke it using its name followed by parentheses `()`. If the function has parameters, you need to provide the corresponding arguments (values) inside the parentheses.

Calling the `greet` function:

Code snippet

```
greet("Bob")  # Output: Hello, Bob!
greet("Charlie") # Output: Hello, Charlie!
```

When you call `greet("Bob")`, the string `"Bob"` is passed as the argument to the `name` parameter of the `greet` function. The code inside `greet` then executes, using this value.

Calling the add function and using its return value:

Code snippet

```
let result: Int = add(5, 3)
print("The sum is:", result)  # Output: The sum is: 8

let another_sum: Int = add(-2, 10)
```

```
print("Another sum:", another_sum) # Output: Another sum: 8
```

In these examples, the `add` function is called with two integer arguments. The function returns their sum, which is then assigned to the variable `result` or `another_sum`.

Functions are essential for organizing your code, making it more modular, readable, and reusable. By breaking down your program into smaller, well-defined functions, you can manage complexity and make your code easier to understand and maintain.

4.2 Passing Arguments and Returning Values

When you define a function, you can specify parameters, which are like placeholders for input values that the function will receive when it's called. When you call the function, you provide arguments, which are the actual values that get assigned to these parameters. Functions can also send back a result to the part of the code that called them using a `return` statement. Let's explore these concepts in more detail:

1. Passing Arguments to Functions:

When you define a function with parameters, you need to provide corresponding arguments when you call that function. The number and type of the arguments you pass should generally match the parameters defined in the function signature.

Positional Arguments: These are the most common type of arguments. When you call a function with positional arguments, the arguments are matched to the parameters in the order they are defined.

Code snippet

```
fn describe_pet(animal_type: String, pet_name: String):
    print("I have a \(animal_type) named \(pet_name).")
```

```
describe_pet("dog", "Buddy")   # "dog" is assigned to animal_type,
"Buddy" to pet_name
describe_pet("cat", "Whiskers") # "cat" is assigned to animal_type,
"Whiskers" to pet_name
```

The order matters here. If you called describe_pet("Buddy", "dog"), the output would be "I have a Buddy named dog.", which is likely not what you intended.

Keyword Arguments: Some languages (and Mojo might follow suit) allow you to pass arguments using the parameter names as keywords. This can make function calls more explicit and readable, especially when a function has many parameters. The order of keyword arguments doesn't typically matter.

Code snippet

```
# Assuming Mojo supports keyword arguments (check
documentation)
# describe_pet(animal_type="hamster", pet_name="Nibbles")
# describe_pet(pet_name="Lucy", animal_type="goldfish")
```

Default Parameter Values: You can define default values for parameters in a function. If an argument for a parameter with a default value is not provided in the function call, the default value is used.

```
fn greet_optional(name: String, greeting: String = "Hello"):
    print("\(greeting), \(name)!")

greet_optional("Alice")        # Uses the default greeting: "Hello, Alice!"
greet_optional("Bob", "Hi")    # Overrides the default: "Hi, Bob!"
```

Variable Number of Arguments (Varargs): Some languages allow a function to accept a variable number of arguments. The syntax for this varies. You might see something like *args or a similar construct that collects extra positional arguments into a tuple or list. Check Mojo's documentation for how it handles this, if at all.

2. Returning Values from Functions:

Functions can optionally return a value back to the caller using the return statement. The type of the value returned should match the ReturnType specified in the function definition (if one was specified).

Returning a Single Value: The most common scenario is returning a single value.

Code snippet

```
fn multiply(a: Int, b: Int) -> Int:
    return a * b

let product: Int = multiply(7, 6)
print("The product is:", product) # Output: The product is: 42
```

Returning Multiple Values (Potentially using Tuples or other structures): Some languages allow functions to return multiple values, often packaged together in a tuple or a similar data structure. You would then unpack these values when you call the function. Check Mojo's capabilities in this area.

Code snippet

```
# Hypothetical Mojo syntax for returning multiple values (check actual syntax)
# fn get_name_and_age(full_name: String) -> (String, Int):
#     let parts = full_name.split(" ") # Assuming split exists
#     let name = parts[0]
#     let age = 30 # Placeholder
#     return (name, age)
#
# let person = get_name_and_age("Alice Smith")
# let name: String = person[0]
```

```
# let age: Int = person[1]
# print("Name:", name, "Age:", age)
```

Functions Without an Explicit Return Value: If a function doesn't have a `return` statement, or if it has a `return` statement without an expression, it typically implicitly returns a special value (like `None` in Python). In Mojo, you'll need to understand how functions without a specified `ReturnType` behave. They usually perform actions (like printing) rather than producing a value.

Code snippet

```
fn print_message(text: String):
    print("Message:", text)
    # No explicit return statement

let result = print_message("Hello")
# What is the value of 'result' here? (Check Mojo's behavior for
void functions)
```

Understanding how to pass arguments to functions allows you to make your functions more versatile and reusable, as they can operate on different data each time they are called. Returning values enables functions to produce results that can be used in other parts of your program, facilitating modular and organized code.

4.3 Understanding Scope: Local vs. Global Variables

The scope of a variable refers to the region of your code where that variable is accessible or can be used.[1] Understanding scope is crucial for avoiding naming conflicts and for ensuring that variables are used correctly within different parts of your program, especially within functions.[2] Mojo, like most languages, distinguishes between local and global variables.

1. Local Variables:

A local variable is a variable that is defined and exists only within a specific block of code, typically inside a function.[3]

Local variables are created when the function is called and are destroyed when the function finishes executing.[4][5]

They cannot be directly accessed or modified from outside the function where they are defined.[6]

If you try to access a local variable from outside its scope, you will usually get an error.

Here's an example in Mojo:

Code snippet

```
fn my_function():
    var local_var: Int = 10
    print("Inside the function:", local_var)

fn main():
```

```
    my_function()
    # The following line would likely cause an error because
local_var is not defined in main's scope
    # print("Outside the function:", local_var)
```

In this code:

local_var is defined inside my_function.[7] Its scope is limited to the body of my_function.[8]

When my_function is called, local_var is created and its value (10) is printed.

Once my_function finishes, local_var is no longer in existence.

If you were to uncomment the print statement in main, Mojo would likely report an error because local_var is not defined within the scope of the main function.

2. Global Variables:

A global variable is a variable that is defined outside of any function (at the top level of your script or module).[9]

Global variables are generally accessible from any part of the code, including inside functions.[10]

They exist for the entire duration of the program's execution.

Here's an example in Mojo:

Code snippet

```
var global_var: String = "I am global"

fn another_function():
    print("Inside another function:", global_var)

fn main():
    print("In main:", global_var)
    another_function()
```

In this code:

`global_var` is defined outside any function, making it a global variable.

It can be accessed and its value can be printed from within the `main` function and also from within `another_function`.[11]

Important Considerations and Potential Pitfalls:

Naming Conflicts: If you have a local variable inside a function with the same name as a global variable, the local variable will "shadow" or hide the global variable within that function's scope. When you use that name inside the function, you will be referring to the local variable, not the global one.

Code snippet

```
var message: String = "Global message"

fn show_message():
    var message: String = "Local message"
    print("Inside function:", message)

fn main():
```

```
print("In main (before call):", message)
show_message()
print("In main (after call):", message)
```

Output would likely be:

```
In main (before call): Global message
Inside function: Local message
In main (after call): Global message
```

Notice that the global `message` and the local `message` in `show_message` are distinct variables. Changes to the local `message` do not affect the global `message`.

Modifying Global Variables from Inside Functions: In many programming languages (including Mojo, likely), if you want to modify a global variable from within a function, you might need to explicitly declare your intention to do so using a keyword (like `global` in Python). Without such a declaration, assigning to a variable with the same name inside a function will typically create a new local variable, rather than modifying the global one.

Code snippet

var counter: Int = 0

fn increment_counter():

```
    # Might need a 'global' keyword here in some languages (check
Mojo's rule)
    global counter  # If Mojo requires this
    counter = counter + 1
    print("Counter inside function:", counter)

fn main():
    print("Counter before:", counter)
    increment_counter()
    print("Counter after:", counter)
```

Without the `global` keyword (if Mojo requires it), the `increment_counter` function might create a local `counter` and not modify the global one. Always refer to Mojo's specific rules on modifying global variables from within functions.

Best Practices: While global variables can sometimes be convenient, excessive use of them can make code harder to understand, debug, and maintain.[12] It can lead to unexpected side effects if a global variable is modified in one part of the program and that change unintentionally affects other parts. It's generally recommended to keep the scope of variables as local as possible and to pass data into and out of functions using parameters and return values. This promotes better code organization and reduces the chances of unintended interactions between different parts of your program.

Understanding scope is fundamental for writing correct and maintainable Mojo code. It helps you manage the lifetime and accessibility of your variables, preventing errors and making your programs more predictable.

CHAPTER 5

Working with Collections: Lists and Tuples

5.1 Introducing Lists: Ordered and Mutable Data Structures

Lists are a fundamental data structure in many programming languages, including what we can expect in Mojo. They are used to store collections of items in a specific order. Two key characteristics define lists:

Ordered: The elements in a list have a specific sequence, and this order is maintained. The position of each item is significant and is identified by an index (starting from 0 for the first element).

Mutable: Mutable means that you can change the contents of a list after it has been created. You can add, remove, or modify elements within the list.

Here's how you might work with lists in Mojo:

1. Creating Lists:

You can create a list by enclosing a sequence of items within square brackets [ ], with the items separated by commas. The items in a list can be of the same data type or, in some dynamically-typed languages, they can be of different types (though it's often good practice to keep them consistent for clarity and predictability).

Code snippet

```
var numbers: List[Int] = [1, 2, 3, 4, 5]
var names: List[String] = ["Alice", "Bob", "Charlie"]
var mixed: List[Any] = [1, "hello", 3.14, true] # If Mojo supports
mixed-type lists

print(numbers) # Output: [1, 2, 3, 4, 5]
print(names)   # Output: ["Alice", "Bob", "Charlie"]
print(mixed)   # Output: [1, "hello", 3.14, true] (if supported)

var empty_list: List[Int] = [] # Creating an empty list
print(empty_list) # Output: []
```

In Mojo, you might need to explicitly specify the type of elements the list will hold (e.g., List[Int], List[String]).

2. Accessing Elements (Indexing):

Because lists are ordered, you can access individual elements using their index. Indices start from 0 for the first element, 1 for the second, and so on. You can also use negative indexing to access elements from the end of the list (-1 for the last element, -2 for the second to last, etc.).

Code snippet

```
var colors: List[String] = ["red", "green", "blue"]

var first_color: String = colors[0]
print(first_color) # Output: red

var second_color: String = colors[1]
print(second_color) # Output: green

var last_color: String = colors[-1]
print(last_color)  # Output: blue
```

3. Modifying Elements:

Being mutable, you can change the value of an element at a specific index:

Code snippet

```
var fruits: List[String] = ["apple", "banana", "cherry"]
fruits[1] = "orange"
print(fruits) # Output: ["apple", "orange", "cherry"]
```

Here, the element at index 1 ("banana") is replaced with "orange".

4. Adding Elements:

Lists provide methods to add new elements:

append(): Adds an element to the end of the list.

Code snippet

```
var animals: List[String] = ["dog", "cat"]
animals.append("elephant")
print(animals) # Output: ["dog", "cat", "elephant"]
```

insert(): Inserts an element at a specific index.

Code snippet

```
var cities: List[String] = ["London", "Tokyo"]
cities.insert(1, "Paris") # Inserts "Paris" at index 1
print(cities) # Output: ["London", "Paris", "Tokyo"]
```

5. Removing Elements:

You can remove elements from a list in several ways:

`remove()`: Removes the first occurrence of a specific value.

Code snippet

```
var numbers_to_remove: List[Int] = [1, 2, 3, 2, 4]
numbers_to_remove.remove(2)
print(numbers_to_remove) # Output: [1, 3, 2, 4] (first '2' is
removed)
```

`pop()`: Removes and returns the element at a specific index. If no index is provided, it removes and returns the last element.

Code snippet

```
var items: List[String] = ["book", "pen", "pencil"]
var removed_item: String = items.pop(1)
print(removed_item) # Output: pen
print(items)     # Output: ["book", "pencil"]

var last_item: String = items.pop()
print(last_item) # Output: pencil
print(items)     # Output: ["book"]
```

`clear()`: Removes all elements from the list, making it empty.

Code snippet

```
var data: List[Int] = [10, 20, 30]
data.clear()
print(data) # Output: []
```

6. Other Common List Operations:

`len()`: Returns the number of elements in the list.

Code snippet

```
var my_list_len: List[Int] = [10, 20, 30, 40]
```

```
var length: Int = len(my_list_len)
print(length) # Output: 4
```

`index()`: Returns the index of the first occurrence of a specific value.

Code snippet

```
var letters: List[String] = ["a", "b", "c", "b"]
var index_of_b: Int = letters.index("b")
print(index_of_b) # Output: 1
```

`count()`: Returns the number of times a specific value appears in the list.

Code snippet

```
var values: List[Int] = [1, 2, 2, 3, 2, 4]
var count_of_2: Int = values.count(2)
print(count_of_2) # Output: 3
```

Slicing: You can extract a sublist (a portion of the list) using slicing.

Code snippet

```
var numbers_slice: List[Int] = [0, 1, 2, 3, 4, 5]
var sublist: List[Int] = numbers_slice[1:4] # Elements from index 1
up to (but not including) 4
print(sublist) # Output: [1, 2, 3]
```

Lists are incredibly versatile and are used extensively in programming to store and manipulate collections of data. Their ordered and mutable nature makes them suitable for a wide range of tasks.

5.2 Exploring Tuples: Ordered and Immutable Data Structures

Tuples are another fundamental data structure used to store collections of items in a specific order, much like lists. However, the key difference between tuples and lists is that **tuples are immutable**. This means that once a tuple is created, you cannot change[1] its contents: you cannot add, remove, or modify elements[2] within it.

Here's how you might work with tuples in Mojo:

1. Creating Tuples:

You create a tuple by enclosing a sequence of items within parentheses ( ), with the items separated by commas.

Code snippet

```
var point: Tuple[Int, Int] = (10, 20)
var person: Tuple[String, Int, String] = ("Alice", 30, "Engineer")
var colors: Tuple[String, String, String] = ("red", "green", "blue")

print(point)  # Output: (10, 20)
print(person) # Output: ("Alice", 30, "Engineer")
print(colors) # Output: ("red", "green", "blue")

var empty_tuple: Tuple[] = () # Creating an empty tuple
print(empty_tuple) # Output: ()

var single_item_tuple: Tuple[String] = ("hello",) # Note the trailing
comma
print(single_item_tuple) # Output: ("hello",)
```

In Mojo, you might need to explicitly specify the types of elements the tuple will hold. Note the special syntax for a single-item tuple – the trailing comma is necessary to distinguish it from a parenthesized expression.

2. Accessing Elements (Indexing):

Like lists, tuples are ordered, so you can access individual elements using their index, starting from 0. Negative indexing also works.

Code snippet

```
var data: Tuple[String, Int] = ("Bob", 25)

var name: String = data[0]
print(name) # Output: Bob
```

```
var age: Int = data[1]
print(age)  # Output: 25

var last_item: String = colors[-1] # Using the 'colors' tuple from
above
print(last_item) # Output: blue
```

3. Immutability:

This is the defining characteristic of tuples. Once a tuple is created, you cannot change its elements. Any attempt to modify a tuple will result in an error.

Code snippet

```
var my_tuple: Tuple[Int, Int] = (1, 2)
# The following lines would cause errors:
# my_tuple[0] = 10
# my_tuple.append(3)
# del my_tuple[1]
```

4. Tuple Unpacking:

A convenient feature of tuples (and often lists as well) is the ability to unpack their elements into individual variables.

Code snippet

```
var coordinates: Tuple[Int, Int] = (5, 12)
var x: Int = coordinates[0]
var y: Int = coordinates[1]
print("x:", x, "y:", y) # Output: x: 5 y: 12

# More concisely with unpacking:
var (a, b): Tuple[Int, Int] = coordinates
```

```
print("a:", a, "b:", b) # Output: a: 5 b: 12
```

```
var person_info: Tuple[String, Int, String] = ("Charlie", 35, "Doctor")
var (name_p, age_p, profession): Tuple[String, Int, String] =
person_info
print("Name:", name_p, "Age:", age_p, "Profession:", profession)
```

5. Common Tuple Operations:

While you can't modify tuples, you can perform certain operations on them:

`len()`: Returns the number of elements in the tuple.

Code snippet

```
var my_tuple_len: Tuple[Int, String, Bool] = (100, "test", true)
var length: Int = len(my_tuple_len)
print(length) # Output: 3
```

Concatenation: You can create a new tuple by concatenating two or more existing tuples using the + operator.

Code snippet

```
var tuple1: Tuple[Int, Int] = (1, 2)
var tuple2: Tuple[Int, Int] = (3, 4)
var combined_tuple: Tuple[Int, Int, Int, Int] = tuple1 + tuple2
```

```
print(combined_tuple) # Output: (1, 2, 3, 4)
```

Repetition: You can repeat the elements of a tuple to create a new tuple using the * operator.

Code snippet

```
var repeat_tuple: Tuple[String] = ("hello",) * 3
print(repeat_tuple) # Output: ("hello", "hello", "hello")
```

Why Use Tuples?

Immutability: The immutability of tuples makes them suitable for representing fixed collections of items, such as coordinates, records, or settings that should not be changed after creation. This can help prevent accidental modifications and make your code more robust.

Performance: In some cases, tuples might be slightly more efficient than lists for collections that you know won't need to be modified.

Data Integrity: Using tuples can signal to other developers (and to yourself) that the data in the collection is intended to be constant.

Use as Keys in Dictionaries (in some languages): Because they are immutable, tuples can often be used as keys in dictionaries, whereas lists (being mutable) cannot. We'll explore dictionaries in the next section.

In summary, tuples are ordered, immutable sequences of items. They are created using parentheses and are useful for representing fixed collections of data. While you cannot modify them after creation, you can access their elements, unpack them, and perform operations like concatenation and repetition.

5.3 Accessing and Manipulating Elements in Collections

Now that we've covered lists and tuples, let's delve into the common ways you can access and manipulate the elements within these ordered collections in Mojo. Keep in mind that while both support accessing elements similarly, manipulation (changing, adding, removing) is primarily for mutable collections like lists.

1. Accessing Elements (Indexing):

Both lists and tuples allow you to access individual elements using their index. Remember that indexing starts at 0 for the first element.

Code snippet

```
var my_list: List[String] = ["apple", "banana", "cherry"]
var my_tuple: Tuple[Int, Bool] = (10, true)

var first_item_list: String = my_list[0]  # Accessing the first element
of the list
print(first_item_list) # Output: apple

var second_item_tuple: Bool = my_tuple[1]  # Accessing the
second element of the tuple
```

```
print(second_item_tuple) # Output: true
```

```
# Negative indexing works for both
var last_item_list: String = my_list[-1] # Last element
print(last_item_list)  # Output: cherry
```

2. Slicing:

Slicing allows you to extract a subsequence of elements from both lists and tuples. You specify a start index, an end index (exclusive), and an optional step.

Code snippet

```
var numbers: List[Int] = [0, 1, 2, 3, 4, 5, 6, 7, 8, 9]
var subset_list: List[Int] = numbers[2:5]   # Elements at indices 2, 3, 4
print(subset_list) # Output: [2, 3, 4]
```

```
var every_other: List[Int] = numbers[::2]  # From start to end with a step of 2
print(every_other) # Output: [0, 2, 4, 6, 8]
```

```
var reversed_tuple: Tuple[Int] = numbers[::-1] # Creating a reversed tuple (original list remains)
print(reversed_tuple) # Output: (9, 8, 7, 6, 5, 4, 3, 2, 1, 0)
```

```
var first_three: Tuple[Int] = tuple(numbers[:3]) # First three elements as a tuple
print(first_three) # Output: (0, 1, 2)
```

3. Manipulating List Elements (Mutable Operations):

These operations are specific to lists because tuples are immutable.

Changing Elements: You can modify an element at a specific index using assignment.

Code snippet

```
var colors_to_change: List[String] = ["red", "green", "blue"]
colors_to_change[1] = "yellow"
print(colors_to_change) # Output: ["red", "yellow", "blue"]
```

Adding Elements:

`append(item)`: Adds `item` to the end of the list.

`insert(index, item)`: Inserts `item` at the specified `index`.

`extend(another_list)`: Appends all elements from `another_list` to the end of the current list.

Code snippet

```
var fruits_add = ["apple"]
fruits_add.append("banana")
print(fruits_add) # Output: ["apple", "banana"]

fruits_add.insert(0, "mango")
```

```
print(fruits_add) # Output: ["mango", "apple", "banana"]

var more_fruits = ["orange", "grape"]
fruits_add.extend(more_fruits)
print(fruits_add) # Output: ["mango", "apple", "banana", "orange", "grape"]
```

Removing Elements:

`remove(value)`: Removes the first occurrence of `value`.

`pop(index)`: Removes and returns the element at `index`. If no index is given, it removes and returns the last element.

`clear()`: Removes all elements from the list.

Code snippet

```
var numbers_remove = [1, 2, 3, 2, 4]
numbers_remove.remove(2)
print(numbers_remove) # Output: [1, 3, 2, 4]

var last_removed = numbers_remove.pop()
print(last_removed)  # Output: 4
print(numbers_remove) # Output: [1, 3, 2]

numbers_remove.clear()
```

```
print(numbers_remove) # Output: []
```

Sorting and Reversing:

`sort()`: Sorts the list in place (modifies the original list).

`reverse()`: Reverses the elements of the list in place.

Code snippet

```
var unsorted_numbers = [3, 1, 4, 1, 5, 9, 2, 6]
unsorted_numbers.sort()
print(unsorted_numbers) # Output: [1, 1, 2, 3, 4, 5, 6, 9]

var letters_reverse = ["a", "b", "c"]
letters_reverse.reverse()
print(letters_reverse) # Output: ["c", "b", "a"]
```

4. Iterating Through Collections:

You can use loops (like the `for` loop we discussed earlier) to iterate over the elements of both lists and tuples.

Code snippet

```
var colors_iterate = ["red", "green", "blue"]
for color in colors_iterate:
    print("Color:", color)

var point_iterate = (10, 20)
for coord in point_iterate:
    print("Coordinate:", coord)

# You can also access elements by index during iteration
for i in range(0, len(colors_iterate)): # Assuming 'len()' works on
lists
    print("Color at index \(i):", colors_iterate[i])
```

Understanding how to access and manipulate elements in lists and how to access elements in tuples is fundamental for working with collections of data in Mojo. The choice between using a list or a tuple often depends on whether you need a mutable or immutable sequence of items.

CHAPTER 6

Beyond the Basics: Dictionaries and Sets

6.1 Working with Dictionaries: Key-Value Pairs

Dictionaries are a powerful and versatile data structure used to store collections of **key-value pairs**. Unlike lists and tuples, which are indexed by a sequence of numbers, dictionaries are indexed by unique keys. These keys are used to quickly access their corresponding values. Dictionaries are often referred to as associative arrays, maps, or hash maps in other programming languages.

Here's how you might work with dictionaries in Mojo:

1. Creating Dictionaries:

You create a dictionary by enclosing key-value pairs within curly braces { }. Each key-value pair is separated by a colon : and pairs are separated by commas , .

Code snippet

```
var ages: Dict[String, Int] = {"Alice": 30, "Bob": 25, "Charlie": 35}
var cities: Dict[String, String] = {"USA": "Washington D.C.", "Nigeria": "Abuja", "Japan": "Tokyo"}
var empty_dict: Dict[String, Int] = {}

print(ages)   # Output: {"Alice": 30, "Bob": 25, "Charlie": 35} (Order might not be guaranteed)
print(cities)  # Output: {"USA": "Washington D.C.", "Nigeria": "Abuja", "Japan": "Tokyo"} (Order might not be guaranteed)
print(empty_dict) # Output: {}
```

In Mojo, you might need to explicitly specify the types of the keys and the values the dictionary will hold (e.g., `Dict[String, Int]`, where keys are strings and values are integers).

2. Accessing Values:

You can access the value associated with a key using square bracket notation, similar to how you access elements in a list or tuple, but instead of an index, you use the key.

Code snippet

```
var student_grades: Dict[String, Float] = {"Math": 90.5, "Science": 85.0, "English": 92.0}

var math_grade: Float = student_grades["Math"]
print("Math grade:", math_grade) # Output: Math grade: 90.5

var science_grade: Float = student_grades["Science"]
print("Science grade:", science_grade) # Output: Science grade: 85.0

# Trying to access a key that doesn't exist will typically result in an error
# var history_grade: Float = student_grades["History"] # This would likely cause an error
```

To avoid errors when a key might not exist, you can use the `get()` method, which returns `None` (or a specified default value) if the key is not found.

Code snippet

```
var student_info: Dict[String, Any] = {"name": "David", "age": 22}

var name_info: String = student_info.get("name")
print("Name:", name_info) # Output: Name: David

var city_info: String? = student_info.get("city") # Assuming optional
type String?
print("City:", city_info) # Output: City: None (or null, depending on
Mojo's null handling)

var default_city: String = student_info.get("city", "Unknown")
print("City (with default):", default_city) # Output: City (with
default): Unknown
```

3. Modifying Dictionaries:

Dictionaries are mutable, meaning you can add new key-value pairs, change the value associated with an existing key, or remove key-value pairs.

Adding New Key-Value Pairs: Simply assign a value to a new key.

Code snippet

```
var phone_numbers: Dict[String, String] = {"Alice": "123-4567"}
phone_numbers["Bob"] = "987-6543"
print(phone_numbers) # Output: {"Alice": "123-4567", "Bob":
"987-6543"}
```

Updating Existing Values: Assign a new value to an existing key.

Code snippet

```
phone_numbers["Alice"] = "111-2222"
print(phone_numbers)  # Output: {"Alice": "111-2222", "Bob": "987-6543"}
```

Removing Key-Value Pairs:

pop(key): Removes the key and returns its associated value. If the key is not found, it raises an error (unless a default value is provided).

del dictionary[key]: Removes the key-value pair with the specified key. If the key is not found, it raises an error.

clear(): Removes all key-value pairs from the dictionary.

Code snippet

```
var scores: Dict[String, Int] = {"Player1": 100, "Player2": 150, "Player3": 120}

var player2_score: Int = scores.pop("Player2")
```

```
print("Popped score:", player2_score) # Output: Popped score:
150
print("Updated scores:", scores)        # Output: {"Player1": 100,
"Player3": 120}

del scores["Player1"]
print("Scores after deletion:", scores) # Output: {"Player3": 120}

scores.clear()
print("Cleared scores:", scores)      # Output: {}
```

4. Common Dictionary Operations:

`len()`: Returns the number of key-value pairs in the dictionary.

Code snippet

```
var items_count: Dict[String, Int] = {"apple": 5, "banana": 3,
"orange": 7}
var count: Int = len(items_count)
print("Number of items:", count) # Output: Number of items: 3
```

`keys()`: Returns a view object that displays a list of all the keys in the dictionary.

Code snippet

```
var my_dict_keys: Dict[String, Int] = {"a": 1, "b": 2, "c": 3}
var keys_view = my_dict_keys.keys()
print("Keys:", keys_view) # Output: ["a", "b", "c"] (Order might vary)
```

values(): Returns a view object that displays a list of all the values in the dictionary.

Code snippet

```
var my_dict_values: Dict[String, Int] = {"a": 1, "b": 2, "c": 3}
var values_view = my_dict_values.values()
print("Values:", values_view) # Output: [1, 2, 3] (Order might vary)
```

items(): Returns a view object that displays a list of all key-value pairs as tuples.

Code snippet

```
var my_dict_items: Dict[String, Int] = {"a": 1, "b": 2, "c": 3}
var items_view = my_dict_items.items()
```

```
print("Items:", items_view) # Output: [("a", 1), ("b", 2), ("c", 3)]
(Order might vary)
```

5. Iterating Through Dictionaries:

You can iterate over the keys, values, or key-value pairs of a dictionary using loops.

Code snippet

```
var product_prices: Dict[String, Float] = {"laptop": 1200.00,
"mouse": 25.00, "keyboard": 75.00}

# Iterate over keys
for product in product_prices.keys():
    print("Product:", product)

# Iterate over values
for price in product_prices.values():
    print("Price:", price)

# Iterate over key-value pairs
for (product, price) in product_prices.items():
    print("\(product) costs $\(price)")
```

Dictionaries are incredibly useful for representing data that has a natural association between keys and values, such as configuration settings, records, or any data where you need to quickly look up a value based on a unique identifier.

6.2 Understanding Sets: Unique and Unordered Collections

Sets are another fundamental data structure in Mojo used to store collections of items.[1] Two key characteristics define sets:

Unique: Sets only store unique elements.[2] If you try to add an element that already exists in the set, it will not be added again.

Unordered: The elements in[3] a set do not have a specific order.[4] You cannot access elements by an index like you do with lists or tuples. The order in which elements appear when you print a set might vary.[5]

Here's how you might work with sets in Mojo:

1. Creating Sets:

You can create a set by enclosing a sequence of items within curly braces {}, similar to dictionaries, but without the key-value pairs.

Code snippet

```
var my_set: Set[Int] = {1, 2, 3, 4, 5}
var colors: Set[String] = {"red", "green", "blue"}
var empty_set: Set[Int] = {} # To create an empty set, use Set[T]()

print(my_set)   # Output: {1, 2, 3, 4, 5} (Order might vary)
print(colors) # Output: {"red", "green", "blue"} (Order might vary)
print(empty_set) # Output: {}
```

In Mojo, you might need to explicitly specify the type of elements the set will hold (e.g., Set[Int], Set[String]). Note that to create an empty set, you typically use the constructor like Set[Int]() rather than just {} which would create an empty dictionary.

2. Adding Elements:

You can add new elements to a set using the add() method.

Code snippet

```
var fruits: Set[String] = {"apple", "banana"}
fruits.add("cherry")
print(fruits) # Output: {"apple", "banana", "cherry"} (Order might vary)

# Adding an existing element has no effect
fruits.add("banana")
print(fruits) # Output: {"apple", "banana", "cherry"} (Order might vary)
```

3. Removing Elements:

You can remove elements from a set using several methods:

remove(element): Removes the specified element from the set. If the element is not found, it will typically raise an error.

discard(element): Removes the specified element if it is present in the set.[6] If the element is not found, it does nothing and does not raise an error.

pop(): Removes and returns an arbitrary element from the set. Since sets are unordered, you don't know which element will be removed. This method will raise an error if the set is empty.

clear(): Removes all elements from the set.

Code snippet

```
var numbers_set: Set[Int] = {1, 2, 3, 4, 5}

numbers_set.remove(3)
print(numbers_set) # Output: {1, 2, 4, 5} (Order might vary)

numbers_set.discard(6) # Does nothing, no error
print(numbers_set) # Output: {1, 2, 4, 5} (Order might vary)

var removed_element: Int = numbers_set.pop()
print("Removed:", removed_element) # Output: Removed: (an
arbitrary element)
print(numbers_set) # Output: (set without the popped element,
order might vary)

numbers_set.clear()
print(numbers_set) # Output: {}
```

4. Common Set Operations:

Sets support various mathematical set operations:

Union (| or `union()`): Returns a new set containing all elements from both sets.

Intersection (& or `intersection()`): Returns a new set containing only the elements that are common to both sets.

Difference (- or `difference()`): Returns a new set containing elements that are in the first set but not in the second set.

Symmetric Difference[7] **(^ or `symmetric_difference()`):** Returns a new set containing elements that are in either of the sets but not in their intersection.[8]

Subset (`<=` or `issubset()`): Checks if all elements of one set are present in another set.

Superset (`>=` or `issuperset()`): Checks if one set contains all elements of another set.

Code snippet

```
var set1: Set[Int] = {1, 2, 3}
var set2: Set[Int] = {3, 4, 5}

var union_set: Set[Int] = set1 | set2
print("Union:", union_set) # Output: {1, 2, 3, 4, 5} (Order might vary)

var intersection_set: Set[Int] = set1 & set2
print("Intersection:", intersection_set) # Output: {3} (Order might vary)

var difference_set: Set[Int] = set1 - set2
print("Difference (set1 - set2):", difference_set) # Output: {1, 2} (Order might vary)

var symmetric_difference_set: Set[Int] = set1 ^ set2
print("Symmetric Difference:", symmetric_difference_set) # Output: {1, 2, 4, 5} (Order might vary)

var is_subset: Bool = {1, 2} <= set1
print("Is {1, 2} a subset of set1?", is_subset) # Output: true

var is_superset: Bool = set2 >= {4, 5}
print("Is set2 a superset of {4, 5}?", is_superset) # Output: true
```

5. Iterating Through Sets:

You can iterate over the elements of a set using a `for` loop.[9] However, remember that the order of iteration is not guaranteed.

Code snippet

```
var letters_set: Set[String] = {"a", "b", "c"}
for letter in letters_set:
    print("Letter:", letter) # Output: (Elements in no particular order)
```

Why Use Sets?

Uniqueness: Sets are very useful when you need to ensure that you only have unique items in a collection, automatically handling duplicates.

Membership Testing: Checking if an element is present in a set is typically very efficient.

Set Operations: Sets provide convenient and efficient ways to perform mathematical set operations like union, intersection, and difference.

In summary, sets are unordered collections of unique elements. They are useful for tasks like removing duplicates, checking for membership, and performing set-related mathematical operations.

6.3 Choosing the Right Collection Type for Your Needs

Selecting the appropriate collection type (list, tuple, dictionary, or set) is crucial for writing efficient and maintainable Mojo code. Each collection type has its own strengths and weaknesses based on its characteristics (ordered, mutable, unique, key-value pairs). Here's a guide to help you choose the right one for different scenarios:

1. Lists (`List[T]`): Ordered and Mutable

Use when:

You need to store a sequence of items, and the order of those items is important.

You need to modify the collection after it's created (add, remove, or change elements).

You might have duplicate items in the collection, and that's acceptable.

You need to access elements by their numerical index.

You plan to iterate through the elements in a specific order.

Examples:

A list of tasks in a to-do application.

A sequence of events in a log file.

A collection of scores for a player in a game, where the order might matter or scores might be added.

A dynamic array where you need to append or remove elements frequently.

2. Tuples (`Tuple[...]`): Ordered and Immutable

Use when:

You need to store a sequence of items, and the order is important, but you don't intend to modify the collection after creation.

You want to ensure data integrity by preventing accidental changes to the collection.

Tuples can sometimes be used as keys in dictionaries (in some languages, check Mojo's rules), unlike lists because they are immutable.

Returning multiple values from a function can often be conveniently done using a tuple.

Representing fixed records of different data types (e.g., a point with x, y coordinates; a person with name, age, city).

Examples:

Representing coordinates (x, y).

Storing RGB color values (red, green, blue).

Returning multiple values from a function.

Configuration settings that should not be altered.

3. Dictionaries (`Dict[KeyType, ValueType]`): **Key-Value Pairs**

Use when:

You need to store data as key-value pairs, where you can quickly retrieve a value based on a unique key.

The order of items is not important (though in some newer language versions, dictionaries might preserve insertion order, but the primary access is by key).

You need to perform lookups, insertions, and deletions based on keys efficiently.

Examples:

Storing user profiles (user ID as key, profile information as value).

Counting the occurrences of words in a text (word as key, count as value).

Configuration settings where each setting has a name (key) and a value.

Mapping product names to their prices.

4. Sets (Set[T]): Unique and Unordered

Use when:

You need to store a collection of unique items, and duplicates are not allowed.

The order of items is not important.

You need to perform set operations like union, intersection, difference, and checking for subsets or supersets efficiently.

You need to quickly check if an element is present in the collection (membership testing).

Examples:

Storing a collection of unique user IDs.

Tracking the unique visitors to a website.

Finding the common elements between two groups of items.

Removing duplicate entries from a list.

Here's a table summarizing the key characteristics:

Feature	List	Tuple	Dictionary	Set
Ordered	Yes	Yes	No (usually)	No
Mutable	Yes	No	Yes	Yes
Duplicates	Allowed	Allowed	Not for keys	Not allowed
Indexing	Numerical index (0-based)	Numerical index (0-based)	By unique key	Not directly indexable
Use Case	Ordered, modifiable data	Fixed, ordered data	Key-value lookups	Unique items, set operations

Questions to Ask Yourself When Choosing:

Do I need to maintain the order of elements? If yes, consider a list or a tuple.

Will I need to modify the collection after it's created? If yes, a list or a set. If no, a tuple might be a better choice for immutability, or a dictionary if you have key-value pairs.

Do I need to ensure that all elements are unique? If yes, a set is the appropriate choice.

Do I need to associate values with unique keys for efficient lookup? If yes, a dictionary is the way to go.

By considering these questions and the characteristics of each collection type, you can make an informed decision about which one is best suited for your specific programming needs in Mojo.

CHAPTER 7

Handling Errors Gracefully: Exception Handling

7.1 Understanding Common Errors and Exceptions

Errors and exceptions are a crucial part of programming. They indicate that something unexpected or problematic has occurred during the execution of your Mojo code. Understanding these concepts is essential for writing robust and reliable programs that can handle issues gracefully.

1. Errors:

Errors typically represent more serious problems that often prevent the program from continuing its normal execution. They can be caused by various factors, including:

Syntax Errors: These occur when your code violates the grammar rules of the Mojo language. The Mojo compiler or interpreter will usually detect these before the program even starts running.

Code snippet

```
# Example of a syntax error (missing colon)
# fn my_function()
#    print("Hello")

# Example of another syntax error (misspelled keyword)
# fun main():
```

```
#    print("World")
```

The Mojo environment will usually provide an error message indicating the location and type of syntax error, which you need to fix before you can run your code.

Logical Errors: These occur when your code is syntactically correct but doesn't produce the intended behavior due to flaws in your program's logic. These errors can be harder to find as they don't necessarily cause the program to crash but lead to incorrect results.

Code snippet

```
# Example of a logical error (incorrect calculation)
fn calculate_average(a: Int, b: Int) -> Float:
    return a + b # Should be (a + b) / 2

fn main():
    let avg = calculate_average(5, 10)
    print("Average:", avg) # Output: 15 (incorrect)
```

Debugging logical errors often involves careful testing and stepping through your code to understand its flow and the values of variables.

2. Exceptions:

Exceptions are events that occur during the execution of a program that disrupt the normal flow of instructions.[1] They are often caused by conditions that your program can potentially handle. Examples include trying to open a file that doesn't exist, dividing by zero, or accessing an index that is out of bounds in a list.

When an exception occurs, Mojo will typically:

1.Stop the current execution of the code.

2. Create an exception object that contains information about the error.

3. Look for code that is designed to "handle" this type of exception. If no such code is found in the current function, it will propagate up the call stack to the function that called it, and so on.

4. If the exception reaches the top level of the program without being handled, the program will usually terminate, and an error message (the traceback) will be displayed, indicating where the exception occurred and the sequence of function calls that led to it.

Common Types of Exceptions You Might Encounter (Mojo might have similar or equivalent types):

ZeroDivisionError: Raised when you attempt to divide a number by zero.

IndexError: Raised when you try to access an index in a sequence (like a list or tuple) that is outside the valid range of indices.

KeyError: Raised when you try to access a key in a dictionary that does not exist.

`FileNotFoundError`: Raised when you try to open a file that cannot be found.

`TypeError`: Raised when an operation or function is applied to an object of an inappropriate type.

`ValueError`: Raised when a function receives an argument of the correct type but an^2 inappropriate value.

Example of Exceptions:

Code snippet

```
fn divide(a: Int, b: Int) -> Float:
    if b == 0:
        # In a real scenario, Mojo might have a way to raise a specific exception
        print("Error: Cannot divide by zero.")
        return Float(0.0) # Or handle differently
    return Float(a) / Float(b)

fn main():
    let result1 = divide(10, 2)
    print("Result 1:", result1) # Output: Result 1: 5.0

    let result2 = divide(5, 0)
    print("Result 2:", result2) # Output: Error: Cannot divide by zero.
Result 2: 0.0
```

In this example, we are manually checking for a potential error (division by zero). However, Mojo provides mechanisms for handling exceptions more formally using `try` and `except` blocks, which we will discuss in the next section.

Understanding the difference between syntax errors, logical errors, and runtime exceptions is crucial for debugging and writing reliable Mojo programs. While syntax errors are usually caught early, logical errors require careful testing, and exceptions need to be handled to prevent your program from crashing unexpectedly.

7.2 Using try and except Blocks to Catch Errors

The try and except blocks in Mojo (and many other languages) provide a mechanism for handling exceptions gracefully. This allows your program to continue running even if an error occurs in a specific section of code. The basic structure is as follows:
Code snippet

```
try:
    # Code that might raise an exception
    # ...
except ExceptionType1:
    # Code to handle ExceptionType1
    # ...
except ExceptionType2:
    # Code to handle ExceptionType2
    # ...
# Optional:
# finally:
#       # Code that will be executed regardless of whether an exception occurred
#    # ...
```

Let's break down each part:

try: **Block:** This block contains the code that you suspect might raise an exception. If an exception occurs within this block, the normal flow of execution is interrupted, and the program looks for a matching `except` block to handle the exception.

`except ExceptionType:` **Block:** This block specifies the type of exception that it can handle (`ExceptionType`). If an exception of this type (or a subclass of it) occurs in the `try` block, the code within this `except` block is executed. You can have multiple `except` blocks to handle different types of exceptions.

`finally:` **Block (Optional):** The `finally` block, if present, contains code that will be executed no matter what happens in the `try` block – whether an exception occurred or not, and whether it was handled by an `except` block or not. It's often used for cleanup operations, like closing files or releasing resources.

How it Works:

1.The code in the `try` block is executed.

2. If no exception occurs in the `try` block, the `except` blocks are skipped, and if there's a `finally` block, it's executed. Then, the program continues with the code after the `try...except...finally` structure.

3. If an exception occurs in the `try` block, the program immediately stops executing the `try` block and looks for an `except` block that matches the type of the exception that occurred.

4. If a matching `except` block is found, the code within that block is executed. After the `except` block finishes, the program

continues with the code after the `try...except...finally` structure (unless the `except` block itself raises an unhandled exception).

5. If no matching `except` block is found, the exception is considered unhandled and will propagate up the call stack. If it reaches the top level without being handled, the program will typically terminate.

6. If a `finally` block is present, the code within it is always executed, regardless of whether an exception occurred in the `try` block and whether it was handled. The `finally` block is executed after the `try` block finishes normally, after an `except` block finishes, or even if an exception occurs that isn't caught.

Examples:

Handling `ZeroDivisionError`:

Code snippet

```
fn safe_divide(a: Int, b: Int) -> Float:
    try:
        return Float(a) / Float(b)
    except ZeroDivisionError:
        print("Error: Cannot divide by zero.")
        return Float(0.0)

fn main():
    let result1 = safe_divide(10, 2)
    print("Result 1:", result1) # Output: Result 1: 5.0

    let result2 = safe_divide(5, 0)
```

print("Result 2:", result2) # Output: Error: Cannot divide by zero.
Result 2: 0.0

In this example, if a `ZeroDivisionError` occurs in the `try` block, the code in the `except ZeroDivisionError` block is executed, printing an error message and returning a default value. The program doesn't crash.

Handling `IndexError`:

Code snippet

```
fn got_lict_item(my_list: List[Int], index· Int) -> Int?: # Assuming
optional return type
    try:
        return my_list[index]
    except IndexError:
        print("Error: Index out of bounds.")
        return None

fn main():
    let numbers = [1, 2, 3]
    let item1 = get_list_item(numbers, 1)
    print("Item at index 1:", item1) # Output: Item at index 1: 2

    let item2 = get_list_item(numbers, 5)
        print("Item at index 5:", item2) # Output: Error: Index out of
bounds. Item at index 5: None
```

Here, if you try to access an index that's out of range, an `IndexError` is caught, an error message is printed, and the function returns `None`.

Using `finally` for Cleanup:

Code snippet

```
fn open_and_read_file(filename: String):
    var file = None # Assuming a file object type
    try:
        file = open(filename, "r") # Hypothetical open function
        let content = file.read()   # Hypothetical read method
        print("File content:", content)
    except FileNotFoundError:
        print("Error: File not found.")
    finally:
        if file is not None:
                file.close() # Ensure the file is closed, even if an error
occurred

fn main():
    open_and_read_file("my_document.txt")
```

In this example, the `finally` block ensures that if the file was opened successfully (or even if an error occurred during opening), the `file.close()` method will be called to release the file resource.

Catching Multiple Exception Types:

You can have multiple `except` blocks to handle different types of exceptions in different ways. You can also catch multiple exceptions in a single `except` block (syntax might vary, e.g., `except (TypeError, ValueError):`).

Best Practices:

Be Specific: Try to catch specific exception types rather than using a generic `except:` (which catches all exceptions). This makes your error handling more targeted and can help you avoid masking unexpected issues.

Handle Errors Appropriately: Decide how your program should respond to different exceptions. Should it print an error message, try a different approach, return a default value, or re-raise the exception?

Use `finally` **for Essential Cleanup:** If you have resources that need to be released (like files, network connections), use the `finally` block to ensure they are cleaned up.

Using `try` and `except` blocks is fundamental for writing programs that can handle runtime errors gracefully and prevent abrupt termination, leading to a better user experience and more reliable software.

7.3 Ensuring Robust Code with finally

The `finally` block in a `try...except...finally` structure plays a crucial role in ensuring the robustness of your Mojo code by providing a guarantee that a certain block of code will always be executed, regardless of what happens in the `try` block (and any associated `except` blocks).

Here's a more detailed look at why `finally` is essential for writing robust code:

1. Guaranteed Execution:

The most important characteristic of the `finally` block is that its code will always run:

If the `try` block completes without raising any exceptions.

If an exception is raised in the `try` block and is caught by an `except` block.

If an exception is raised in the `try` block and is *not* caught by any `except` block (in which case, the exception propagates up the call stack after the `finally` block executes).

Even if a `return`, `break`, or `continue` statement is encountered within the `try` or `except` blocks.

This guarantee makes `finally` indispensable for cleanup operations that must occur to prevent resource leaks or maintain the program's state.

2. Resource Management:

A primary use case for `finally` is managing resources such as:

Files: When you open a file, it's crucial to close it after you're done, even if an error occurred while reading or writing. Failing to close files can lead to data corruption or prevent other processes from accessing them.

Code snippet

```
fn process_file(filename: String):
    var file = None
    try:
        file = open(filename, "r")
        let content = file.read()
        # Process the content
        print("File content:", content)
    except FileNotFoundError:
```

```
        print("Error: File not found.")
    except Exception as e: # Catch other potential errors
        print("An error occurred:", e)
    finally:
        if file is not None:
            file.close()
            print("File closed.")

fn main():
    process_file("data.txt")
```

In this example, the `finally` block ensures that if `open()` was successful, `file.close()` will be called, regardless of whether the file was read without errors or if a `FileNotFoundError` or some other exception occurred during processing.

Network Connections: Similar to files, network connections need to be closed to free up resources and ensure proper communication termination.

Locks and Synchronization Primitives: In concurrent programming, locks are used to control access to shared resources. The `finally` block can ensure that a lock is released, even if an error occurs while the lock is held, preventing deadlocks.

Database Connections: Database connections also need to be closed properly to release resources and avoid connection pool exhaustion.

3. Ensuring Program State:

Sometimes, you need to ensure that certain actions happen to maintain the program's state, regardless of errors. For example, you might need to revert a transaction or update a status flag.

Code snippet

```
fn perform_transaction():
    var transaction_active: Bool = false
    try:
        start_transaction()
        transaction_active = true
        # Perform database operations
        commit_transaction()
        transaction_active = false
        print("Transaction committed successfully.")
    except Exception as e:
        if transaction_active:
            rollback_transaction()
            transaction_active = false
            print("Transaction rolled back due to error:", e)
        else:
            print("Error during transaction setup:", e)
    finally:
        # Any final logging or state updates
        print("Transaction process finished.")

fn main():
    perform_transaction()
```

In this (conceptual) example, the `finally` block ensures that "Transaction process finished." is always printed, providing a consistent log message regardless of the outcome of the transaction.

4. Interaction with `return`, `break`, and `continue`:

Even if a control flow statement like `return`, `break`, or `continue` is executed within the `try` or `except` blocks, the `finally` block will still be executed before the function or loop actually exits. This ensures that cleanup code runs even in these scenarios.

Code snippet

```
fn example_return():
   try:
      print("Inside try")
      return 10
   finally:
      print("Inside finally")

fn main():
   let result = example_return()
   print("Result:", result)
```

Output:

```
Inside try
Inside finally
Result: 10
```

As you can see, "Inside finally" is printed before the function returns.

In Summary:

The `finally` block is a powerful tool for ensuring that critical cleanup code is always executed, making your Mojo programs more robust and less prone to resource leaks or inconsistent state.

By using `finally` appropriately, you can handle errors more gracefully and maintain the integrity of your application.

When you are working with resources that need to be managed (like files, connections, locks), always consider using a `try...except...finally` structure to ensure proper cleanup, regardless of whether errors occur. This is a fundamental principle of writing reliable and robust code.

CHAPTER 8

The Power of Modularity: Modules and Libraries

8.1 Understanding Modules: Organizing Your Code into Files

As your Mojo projects grow in complexity, it becomes essential to organize your code into multiple files. This practice, known as using **modules**, offers several significant benefits for code management, reusability, and maintainability.

What are Modules?

A module is essentially a separate file containing Mojo code (definitions of functions, classes, variables, etc.) that can be imported and used in other Mojo files. Modules help you break down a large program into smaller, more manageable, and logically grouped units.

Benefits of Using Modules:

Organization: Modules allow you to structure your project in a clear and hierarchical way, grouping related code together. This makes it easier to navigate and understand the codebase.

Reusability: Code defined in a module can be easily reused in multiple parts of the same project or even in different projects, reducing redundancy and promoting efficiency.

Maintainability: Changes and bug fixes in one module are less likely to affect other parts of the program, making maintenance and updates easier.

Namespace Management: Modules create separate namespaces, which helps to avoid naming conflicts between identifiers (like function or variable names) defined in different parts of your code.

How Modules Work in Mojo (Conceptual):

While the exact syntax and mechanisms for modules in Mojo are still evolving, the general principles from other languages like Python are likely to apply. Here's a conceptual overview:

1.Creating a Module: You create a module by simply saving Mojo code in a file with a `.mojo` extension (or potentially another extension designated for modules). The name of the file (without the extension) becomes the name of the module.

2. For example, if you have a file named `math_operations.mojo` containing the following code:

3. Code snippet

```
fn add(x: Int, y: Int) -> Int:
    return x + y

fn subtract(x: Int, y: Int) -> Int:
    return x - y

var PI: Float = 3.14159
```
4.

5. Then `math_operations` is a module.

6. Importing a Module: To use the code from a module in another Mojo file, you need to import it using an `import` statement.

7. Code snippet

```
# In another file, say 'main.mojo'
import math_operations

fn main():
    let sum = math_operations.add(5, 3)
    print("Sum:", sum) # Output: Sum: 8

    let difference = math_operations.subtract(10, 4)
    print("Difference:", difference) # Output: Difference: 6

    print("Value of PI:", math_operations.PI) # Output: Value of PI:
3.14159
```
8.

9. Here, `import math_operations` makes the `math_operations` module available in `main.mojo`. You can then access the functions and variables defined in `math_operations` using the module name as a prefix (e.g., `math_operations.add`).

10. Selective Imports: You might not always need to import everything from a module. Many languages allow you to import specific names from a module using a `from ... import ...` syntax. Mojo might support something similar:

11. Code snippet

```
# Hypothetical syntax (check Mojo docs)
# from math_operations import add, PI

# fn main():
#     let sum = add(5, 3)
#     print("Sum:", sum) # Output: Sum: 8
#     print("Value of PI:", PI) # Output: Value of PI: 3.14159
```
12.

13. This imports only the add function and the PI variable directly into the current namespace, so you can use them without the math_operations. prefix.

14. Module Search Path: When you import a module, the Mojo runtime needs to know where to find the corresponding file. There's typically a defined set of directories (the module search path) that the runtime will search in. This path usually includes the current directory, standard library locations, and potentially other directories configured in the environment.

15. Packages (Hierarchical Modules): For very large projects, modules can be further organized into packages, which are essentially directories containing module files (and often a special __init__ file in Python-like systems to mark the directory as a package). This allows for a hierarchical structure of your codebase (e.g., myproject/utils/string_helpers.mojo). Imports for packages might look like import myproject.utils.string_helpers.

Organizing Your Project:

A typical Mojo project might have a structure like this:

```
my_project/
├── main.mojo       # The main entry point of the program
├── utils/
│   ├── math_operations.mojo
│   └── string_helpers.mojo
├── data/
│   └── data_processing.mojo
└── ...
```

In `main.mojo`, you would import the necessary modules:

Code snippet

```
import utils.math_operations
import utils.string_helpers
import data.data_processing

fn main():
    let result = utils.math_operations.add(10, 5)
    let formatted_string = utils.string_helpers.capitalize("hello")
    data.data_processing.load_and_process_data()
    # ...
```

As Mojo evolves, its module system will become clearer. However, the fundamental principles of organization, reusability, and namespace management that modules provide are universal and essential for building scalable and maintainable software.

When you start working on larger Mojo projects, think about how you can logically divide your code into modules based on functionality or purpose. This will greatly improve the structure and maintainability of your codebase.

8.2 Importing and Using Existing Libraries

Leveraging existing libraries is a cornerstone of efficient software development. Libraries are collections of pre-written code (often organized into modules) that provide ready-to-use functionalities for various tasks. Mojo, while still evolving, will undoubtedly have its own standard library and the ability to import and use external libraries.

Here's a conceptual overview of how importing and using existing libraries might work in Mojo, drawing parallels from other languages:

1. The Standard Library:

Most programming languages come with a standard library, which is a set of built-in modules and functions that provide essential functionalities without needing external installation. These often include modules for:

Input/Output operations (reading from and writing to files, console input/output).

Operating system interactions (e.g., file system operations, environment variables).

Networking (making HTTP requests, working with sockets).

Data structures and algorithms (beyond the basic lists, dictionaries, sets).

Date and time manipulation.

Mathematical functions.

When you install the Mojo SDK, it will likely include a standard library. You would import modules from this library using the `import` statement, similar to how you'd import your own modules.

Code snippet

```
# Hypothetical example using a standard library module for file I/O
import io.files

fn main():
    let filename = "example.txt"
    let content = "Hello, Mojo!"
    files.write_text(filename, content)
    let read_content = files.read_text(filename)
    print("Read from file:", read_content)
```

2. External Libraries (Packages):

Beyond the standard library, you'll often need to use third-party libraries (also known as packages or crates in some ecosystems) that provide more specialized functionalities. These libraries are typically developed and maintained by the broader programming community and are often hosted on package repositories.

To use an external library in Mojo, you'll likely need a way to:

Find and Discover Libraries: You'll need to know what libraries are available for the tasks you want to perform. This often involves searching online package repositories or community forums.

Install Libraries: You'll need a package manager tool to download and install these libraries and their dependencies on your system. For Mojo, this might be a tool provided by Modular (the company behind Mojo) or a community-driven solution. For example, a command-line tool might be used like:

Bash

```bash
# Hypothetical Mojo package manager command
mojo package install requests
```

Import and Use Libraries: Once installed, you'll use the `import` statement in your Mojo code to make the library's modules and functions available.

Code snippet

```
# Hypothetical example using an external 'requests' library for
making HTTP requests
import requests

fn main():
    let response = requests.get("https://api.example.com/data")
    if response.status_code == 200:
        let data = response.json()
        print("Data from API:", data)
    else:
        print("Error fetching data:", response.status_code)
```

3. Ways to Import:

As mentioned earlier, you'll likely have different ways to import modules and their contents:

`import module_name`: Imports the entire module. You access its members using the module name as a prefix (e.g., `module_name.function()`).

`from module_name import name1, name2, ...`: Imports specific names (functions, classes, variables) directly into the current namespace, so you can use them without the module prefix (e.g., `function()`).

`from module_name import *`: Imports all public names from the module into the current namespace. While convenient, this can lead to namespace pollution and potential naming conflicts, so it's often discouraged for larger modules.

`import module_name as alias`: Imports the module with a shorter alias, which can be useful for long module names or to avoid conflicts (e.g., `import very_long_module_name as vlm`).

4. Discovering Library Functionality:

Once you've imported a library, you'll need to know how to use its functions and classes. This typically involves:

Reading the Library's Documentation: Most well-maintained libraries provide documentation that explains their purpose, how to install them, and how to use their various components with examples.

Using IDE Features: Integrated Development Environments (IDEs) often provide features like code completion and help tooltips that can show you the available functions and their parameters within an imported module.

Exploring the Module (Carefully): In some cases, you might be able to explore the contents of a module directly in an interactive Mojo environment (if available) or by examining the source code (if it's accessible). However, relying on documentation is generally the best approach.

As the Mojo ecosystem develops, the process of finding, installing, and using libraries will become more defined and streamlined. For now, understanding these general concepts will help you prepare for how you'll likely interact with existing code in Mojo projects.

Keep an eye on the official Modular documentation and community resources for updates on package management and available libraries for Mojo.

8.3 Exploring the Standard Library: Useful Built-in Modules

As mentioned earlier, the standard library of a programming language provides a wealth of pre-built modules that offer essential functionalities.[1] While Mojo's standard library is still evolving, we can anticipate it will include modules similar to those found in other modern languages, especially Python, given Mojo's aim for Python compatibility and ease of use.

Here are some categories of useful built-in modules that you might expect to find in Mojo's standard library:

1. Input/Output (I/O):

File I/O: Modules for reading from and writing to files on the file system. This would allow you to work with text files, binary files, and potentially more structured formats.

Console I/O: Functions for interacting with the user via the command line (e.g., printing output, reading input).

2. Operating System (OS) Interaction:

Modules to interact with the underlying operating system, such as:

File and directory manipulation (creating, deleting, renaming files and directories).

Getting information about the operating system.

Running external commands.

Working with environment variables.[2]

Basic process management.

3. Networking:

Modules for network-related tasks, such as:

Making HTTP requests (for interacting with web services).

Working with sockets (for lower-level network communication).

Handling URLs.

4. Data Structures and Algorithms:

While Mojo has built-in lists, tuples, dictionaries, and sets, the standard library might offer more advanced data structures (e.g., queues, heaps, deques) and algorithms (e.g., sorting, searching).

5. Date and Time:

Modules for working with dates, times, and time intervals. This would include functionalities for:

Getting the current date and time.

Formatting dates and times in various ways.

Performing calculations with dates and times.

Handling time zones.

6. Mathematics:

Modules providing mathematical functions beyond the basic arithmetic operators, such as:

Trigonometric functions (sin, cos, tan).[3]

Logarithmic and exponential functions.

Square root, power.[4]

Constants (e.g., pi, e).

Random number generation.[5]

7. Text Processing:

Modules for working with text data, including:

String manipulation beyond basic operations (e.g., regular expressions for pattern matching).

Text encoding and decoding.

Working with different text formats (e.g., CSV, JSON, XML).

8. Concurrency and Parallelism:

Given Mojo's focus on performance, the standard library might include modules to support concurrent and parallel programming, allowing you to take advantage of multi-core processors.[6] This could involve:

Threads or similar mechanisms for running code concurrently.[7]

Tools for managing shared resources and avoiding race conditions.[8]

9. Utilities and Other Modules:

Various utility modules for common tasks, such as:

Command-line argument parsing.

Logging.

Working with data serialization formats (like JSON).

Example of Potential Standard Library Usage (Conceptual):

Let's imagine Mojo's standard library has a module called `time` for working with time and a module called `math` for mathematical functions:

Code snippet

```
import time
import math

fn main():
    let current_time = time.now()
    print("Current time:", current_time)

    time.sleep(2.0) # Pause execution for 2 seconds
    print("Woke up!")

    let square_root_of_16 = math.sqrt(16.0)
    print("Square root of 16:", square_root_of_16)

    let pi_value = math.pi
    print("Value of pi:", pi_value)
```

How to Discover and Use Standard Library Modules:

Official Mojo Documentation: The primary resource for learning about Mojo's standard library will be the official documentation provided by Modular. This documentation will detail the available modules, their functions, classes, and how to use them.

Community Resources: As the Mojo community grows, tutorials, blog posts, and forums will likely provide examples and guidance on using standard library modules.

IDE Features: IDEs with Mojo support might offer features like code completion and documentation lookups for standard library modules.[9]

As you learn Mojo, it will be beneficial to explore the standard library to see what built-in tools are available. This can save you a significant amount of time and effort by providing ready-made solutions for common programming tasks. Keep an eye on the official Mojo resources for the most up-to-date information on its standard library.

CHAPTER 9

Object-Oriented Principles: Classes and Objects (Introduction)

9.1 Introducing the Concept of Objects and Classes

Now we're moving into the realm of Object-Oriented Programming (OOP), a powerful paradigm that structures software design around "objects" and "classes." Understanding these concepts is crucial for building more complex and organized applications in Mojo.

1. Objects:

At its core, an **object** is a self-contained entity that bundles together:

Data (Attributes or Properties): These are the characteristics or information that describe the object. They are like variables associated with the object. For example, a Car object might have attributes like color, make, model, and speed.

Behavior (Methods): These are the actions or operations that the object can perform. They are like functions associated with the object. For example, a Car object might have methods like start(), accelerate(), brake(), and honk().

Think of a real-world object, like a specific car you see on the street. It has certain properties (its color, make, model) and it can perform certain actions (start, move, stop). In OOP, we model these real-world entities as software objects.

2. Classes:

A **class** is a blueprint or a template for creating objects. It defines the structure and behavior that all objects of that class will share.[1] You can think of a class as a cookie cutter, and the objects (also called instances) are the cookies created using that cutter.

The class specifies:

What attributes an object of that class will have: It defines the names and (often) the types of the data that each object will store.

What methods an object of that class can perform: It defines the functions that can operate on the object's data.

Analogy:

Class: The blueprint for a house. It specifies the number of rooms, the layout, the materials to be used, etc.

Object (Instance): A specific house built from that blueprint. It has its own address, its own occupants, and its own specific state of repair, but it follows the general design defined in the blueprint.

How Classes and Objects Relate in Mojo (Conceptual):

While Mojo's OOP features are still under development, the syntax might resemble other modern languages. Here's a conceptual example of defining a Car class and creating Car objects:

Code snippet

```
# Defining a class named 'Car'
class Car:
    # Attributes (properties) defined in the class
    var color: String
    var make: String
```

```
    var model: String
    var speed: Int

    # Constructor (a special method to initialize objects)
    fn __init__(inout self, color: String, make: String, model: String):
        self.color = color
        self.make = make
        self.model = model
        self.speed = 0

    # Method (behavior) defined in the class
    fn accelerate(inout self, increment: Int):
        self.speed = self.speed + increment
            print("\(self.make) \(self.model) accelerating to \(self.speed)
km/h")

    fn brake(inout self, decrement: Int):
        if self.speed >= decrement:
            self.speed = self.speed - decrement
                print("\(self.make) \(self.model) braking to \(self.speed)
km/h")
        else:
            self.speed = 0
            print("\(self.make) \(self.model) has stopped.")

# Creating objects (instances) of the 'Car' class
fn main():
    let my_car = Car("red", "Toyota", "Camry")
    let another_car = Car("blue", "Honda", "Civic")

    # Accessing attributes of the objects
            print("My  car  is  a  \(my_car.color)  \(my_car.make)
\(my_car.model)")
    print("Another car is a \(another_car.color) \(another_car.make)
\(another_car.model)")
```

```
# Calling methods on the objects
my_car.accelerate(20)
my_car.accelerate(30)
my_car.brake(10)
another_car.accelerate(15)
another_car.brake(20)
```

In this conceptual example:

We define a `Car` class with attributes (`color`, `make`, `model`, `speed`) and methods (`__init__` - the constructor, `accelerate`, `brake`).

The `__init__` method is a special method that gets called when you create a new `Car` object. It initializes the object's attributes. The `self` parameter refers to the instance of the class being created. The `inout self` likely indicates that the method can modify the object's state.

The `accelerate` and `brake` methods define the behavior of `Car` objects, allowing them to change their `speed` and print messages.

In the `main` function, we create two `Car` objects (`my_car` and `another_car`) using the `Car()` constructor, passing initial values for their attributes.

We then access the attributes of these objects using the dot notation (`my_car.color`) and call their methods (`my_car.accelerate(20)`).

Key Principles of OOP:

Object-Oriented Programming is built upon several key principles:

Encapsulation: Bundling data (attributes) and the methods that operate on that data within a single unit (an object). This helps in hiding the internal implementation details of an object and exposing only a well-defined interface.

Abstraction: Simplifying complex reality by modeling only the essential attributes and behaviors of an object relevant to the current context. It focuses on "what" an object does rather than "how" it does it.

Inheritance: A mechanism that allows a new class (subclass or derived class) to inherit properties and behaviors from an existing class[2] (superclass or base class). This promotes code reuse and the creation of hierarchies[3] of related classes.

Polymorphism: The ability of objects of different classes to respond to the same method call in their own way. This allows for more flexible and adaptable code.

As Mojo develops its OOP capabilities, understanding these fundamental concepts of objects and classes will be essential for leveraging its power to build structured and maintainable software.

9.2 Defining Simple Classes and Creating Objects

Building upon the introduction to objects and classes, let's walk through the process of defining a simple class in Mojo and then creating objects (instances) of that class. We'll use a straightforward example to illustrate the basic syntax and concepts.

Conceptual Syntax in Mojo (Subject to Change):

Given Mojo's ongoing development, the exact syntax for classes might evolve. However, it's likely to draw inspiration from languages like Python and have a structure similar to what we outlined before.

1. Defining a Class:

You define a class using the `class` keyword, followed by the name of the class (typically capitalized), and a colon. The body of the class (attributes and methods) is indented under the class definition.

Code snippet

```
class Dog:
    # Attributes (properties)
    var name: String
    var breed: String
    var age: Int

    # Constructor (__init__ method)
    fn __init__(inout self, name: String, breed: String, age: Int):
        self.name = name
        self.breed = breed
        self.age = age

    # Method (behavior)
    fn bark(self):
        print("\(self.name) says Woof!")

    fn describe(self):
        print("\(self.name) is a \(self.age)-year-old \(self.breed).")
```

In this Dog class definition:

class Dog :: This line declares a new class named Dog.

var name: String, var breed: String, var age: Int: These are attribute declarations. They specify that each Dog object will have a name (a string), a breed (a string), and an age (an integer). The var keyword suggests these attributes can be modified after the object is created.

fn __init__(inout self, name: String, breed: String, age: Int):: This is the constructor method. It's a special method that gets called automatically when you create a new Dog object.

self: This is a convention (similar to this in other languages) that refers to the instance of the Dog class being created. The inout likely indicates that this method can modify the self object's attributes.

name: String, breed: String, age: Int: These are parameters that will receive the initial values provided when a Dog object is created.

Inside __init__, we assign the passed-in values to the object's attributes using self.attribute_name = parameter_name.

fn bark(self):: This is a method named bark. It defines an action that a Dog object can perform. The self parameter is automatically passed when you call this method on an object. Inside the method, self.name accesses the name attribute of the specific Dog object that is barking.

`fn describe(self)`:: This is another method named `describe` that prints a description of the `Dog` object using its attributes.

2. Creating Objects (Instances) of the Class:

To use the `Dog` class, you need to create objects (instances) of it. You do this by calling the class name like a function, passing in the initial values for the parameters defined in the `__init__` constructor.

Code snippet

```
fn main():
    # Creating Dog objects
    let my_dog = Dog("Buddy", "Golden Retriever", 3)
    let another_dog = Dog("Lucy", "Poodle", 5)

    # Accessing attributes of the objects
    print("My dog's name:", my_dog.name)   # Output: My dog's name: Buddy
    print("Another dog's breed:", another_dog.breed) # Output: Another dog's breed: Poodle

    # Calling methods on the objects
    my_dog.bark()      # Output: Buddy says Woof!
    another_dog.describe() # Output: Lucy is a 5-year-old Poodle.

    # Modifying attributes (since they were declared with 'var')
    my_dog.age = 4
    my_dog.describe()   # Output: Buddy is a 4-year-old Golden Retriever.
```

In the `main` function:

`let my_dog = Dog("Buddy", "Golden Retriever", 3)`: This line creates a new object of the Dog class. The `Dog()` call invokes the `__init__` method with the provided arguments. The newly created Dog object is assigned to the variable `my_dog`. The `let` keyword suggests that while the attributes of `my_dog` might be mutable (due to `var` in the class), the `my_dog` variable itself might be reassigned depending on Mojo's mutability rules for `let`.

`let another_dog = Dog("Lucy", "Poodle", 5)`: This creates another Dog object and assigns it to `another_dog`.

We then access the attributes of these objects using the dot notation (e.g., `my_dog.name`).

We call the methods on the objects using the dot notation as well (e.g., `my_dog.bark()`). The `self` parameter is automatically handled when you call a method on an object.

Since the `age` attribute was declared with `var` in the Dog class, we can modify its value directly using assignment (`my_dog.age = 4`).

This simple example demonstrates the fundamental steps in defining a class and creating objects from it in Mojo. Classes serve as blueprints, and objects are the concrete instances that embody the attributes and behaviors defined by their class. As you delve deeper into OOP, you'll explore more advanced concepts like inheritance and polymorphism, which build upon this foundation.

9.3 Understanding Attributes and Methods

In the context of Object-Oriented Programming (OOP) in Mojo, **attributes** and **methods** are the fundamental building blocks that define the characteristics and behavior of objects created from a class. Let's break down each concept in detail:

1. Attributes (Properties):

Definition: Attributes are variables that are associated with an object. They store the data or state of the object. In essence, they are the "nouns" that describe an object.

Declaration: Within a class definition, you declare attributes using keywords like `var` or `let` (depending on whether they should be mutable or immutable after object creation), followed by the attribute name and its type (if explicitly specified).

Initialization: Attributes are often initialized within the constructor (`__init__` method) of the class. This sets the initial state of the object when it is created. However, they can also be initialized with default values directly in the class definition.

Accessing Attributes: You access the attributes of an object using the dot notation (`object.attribute_name`).

Mutability: If an attribute is declared with `var`, its value can be changed after the object is created. If declared with `let` (assuming Mojo supports this for class attributes), its value would be fixed after initialization.

Example (Continuing with the `Dog` class):

Code snippet

```
class Dog:
    # Attributes
    var name: String
    let breed: String  # Immutable breed
    var age: Int = 0   # Initialized with a default value
```

```
    # Constructor
    fn __init__(inout self, name: String, breed: String, age: Int):
        self.name = name
        self.breed = breed
        self.age = age

    # Method
    fn bark(self):
        print("\(self.name) says Woof!")

    fn birthday(inout self):
        self.age = self.age + 1
        print("\(self.name) is now \(self.age) years old!")

fn main():
    let my_dog = Dog("Buddy", "Golden Retriever", 3)

    # Accessing attributes
    print("Name:", my_dog.name)   # Output: Name: Buddy
        print("Breed:", my_dog.breed) # Output: Breed: Golden
Retriever
    print("Age:", my_dog.age)     # Output: Age: 3

    # Modifying a mutable attribute
    my_dog.name = "Super Buddy"
     print("New name:", my_dog.name) # Output: New name: Super
Buddy

        # The 'breed' attribute is immutable (declared with 'let',
conceptually)
    # my_dog.breed = "Labrador" # This would likely cause an error

    # Calling a method that modifies an attribute
    my_dog.birthday() # Output: Super Buddy is now 4 years old!
```

```
print("Updated age:", my_dog.age) # Output: Updated age: 4
```

In this example:

name, breed, and age are attributes of the Dog class.

name and age are declared with var, making them mutable.

breed is conceptually declared with let, making it immutable after the Dog object is created.

age is initialized with a default value of 0 in the class definition, but this can be overridden in the constructor.

We access these attributes using my_dog.name, my_dog.breed, and my_dog.age.

We can change the value of my_dog.name and my_dog.age because they are mutable.

An attempt to change my_dog.breed would likely result in an error due to its immutability.

2. Methods (Behavior):

Definition: Methods are functions that are associated with an object. They define the actions or operations that an object can perform and can operate on the object's attributes. In essence, they are the "verbs" associated with an object.

Declaration: Methods are defined within a class using the fn keyword, just like regular functions, but they always have at least one parameter: `self`. This `self` parameter is a reference to the instance of the class on which the method is being called.

Accessing Methods: You call a method on an object using the dot notation (`object.method_name(arguments)`). The `self` parameter is automatically passed when you call the method.

Modifying Object State: Methods can access and modify the attributes of the object (using `self.attribute_name`) to change the object's state.

Example (Revisiting the `Dog` class):

Code snippet

```
class Dog:
    var name: String
    let breed: String
    var age: Int

    fn __init__(inout self, name: String, breed: String, age: Int):
        self.name = name
        self.breed = breed
        self.age = age

    # Methods
    fn bark(self):
        print("\(self.name) says Woof!")

    fn birthday(inout self):
        self.age = self.age + 1
        print("\(self.name) is now \(self.age) years old!")

    fn greet(self, other_dog: Dog):
        print("\(self.name) wags its tail at \(other_dog.name).")
```

```
fn main():
    let buddy = Dog("Buddy", "Golden Retriever", 3)
    let lucy = Dog("Lucy", "Poodle", 5)

    # Calling methods
    buddy.bark()       # Output: Buddy says Woof!
    lucy.birthday()    # Output: Lucy is now 6 years old!
    buddy.greet(lucy)  # Output: Buddy wags its tail at Lucy.
```

In this example:

bark, birthday, and greet are methods of the Dog class.

Each method has self as its first parameter, allowing it to access the attributes of the Dog object on which it's called.

The birthday method modifies the age attribute.

The greet method takes another Dog object as an argument (other_dog) and can interact with its attributes as well.

Attributes are the data that an object holds, while methods are the actions that an object can perform, often using or modifying its attributes. Together, they encapsulate the state and behavior of objects, which is a core principle of Object-Oriented Programming.

CHAPTER 10

Your Next Steps with Mojo: Beyond the Basics

10.1 Exploring Mojo's Performance Capabilities

Mojo's performance capabilities are one of its most compelling aspects, especially for developers coming from Python who need more speed without sacrificing ease of use.[1] Mojo aims to bridge the gap between the high-performance world of languages like C++ and the accessibility of Python.[2] Here's a breakdown of how Mojo achieves this:

1. Static Typing and Compile-Time Optimizations:

Static Typing: Unlike Python's dynamic typing (where the type of a variable is checked at runtime), Mojo is designed with static typing (though it often allows for type inference).[3] This means that the types of variables are known at compile time.[4] This allows the Mojo compiler to perform significant optimizations that are impossible in dynamically typed languages.

Compile-Time Optimizations: With static type information, the Mojo compiler can perform various optimizations such as:

Eliminating runtime type checks: Since types are known beforehand, the overhead of checking types during execution is reduced.[5]

Inlining functions: Small function calls can be replaced with the actual function code, reducing function call overhead.[6]

Aggressive loop optimizations: The compiler can analyze loops more effectively and apply optimizations like vectorization (performing operations on multiple data elements simultaneously).[7]

Specialized code generation: The compiler can generate machine code that is highly optimized for the specific data types being used.[8]

2. Ownership and Borrowing (Memory Management):

Mojo incorporates concepts from systems programming languages like Rust, particularly **ownership** and **borrowing**.[9] While the exact implementation in Mojo might differ, the underlying principles aim to provide memory safety and efficient memory management without the need for a garbage collector.

Ownership: Typically, a value in Mojo has a variable that's its "owner." There can only be one owner at a time. When the owner goes out of scope, the value is automatically dropped[10] (deallocated).

Borrowing: Instead of transferring ownership, you can create references (borrows) to a value. Borrowing allows other parts of the code to access the value without taking ownership. Borrowing has rules (e.g., multiple immutable borrows are allowed, but only one mutable borrow at a time within a certain scope) that are checked at compile time to prevent data races and other memory-related issues.

Benefits for Performance: This system can lead to more predictable and efficient memory usage compared to garbage collection, which can introduce pauses during runtime.[11] It also helps prevent common memory errors like dangling pointers.[12]

3. First-Class Metaprogramming:

Mojo is designed with first-class metaprogramming capabilities. This allows you to write code that can inspect and manipulate other code at compile time.

Compile-Time Functions and Code Generation: Metaprogramming enables you to generate specialized code based on types or other compile-time information.[13] This can lead to highly optimized code tailored to specific use cases.

Example: You might be able to write a generic function that, through metaprogramming, generates highly optimized versions for different numeric types.

4. Integration with Hardware (MLIR):

Mojo leverages the **Multi-Level Intermediate Representation (MLIR)**, a compiler infrastructure project.[14] MLIR provides a flexible way to represent code at different levels of abstraction, allowing for optimizations across various hardware targets (CPUs, GPUs, specialized accelerators).[15]

Hardware Acceleration: By using MLIR, Mojo can potentially target and optimize code for specific hardware, leading to significant performance gains for computationally intensive tasks, especially in areas like machine learning.[16]

5. Python Interoperability with Potential Performance Benefits:

Mojo aims for seamless interoperability with Python.[17] This means you can call Python code from Mojo and vice versa.

Gradual Adoption: This interoperability allows Python developers to gradually adopt Mojo, potentially rewriting performance-critical sections of their code in Mojo to gain speedups while still leveraging the vast Python ecosystem.[18]

Optimized Python Integration: While interacting with Python might introduce some overhead, Mojo could potentially optimize these interactions compared to traditional methods of calling native code from Python.

In Summary, Mojo's performance comes from a combination of:

Static typing enabling aggressive compile-time optimizations.[19]

A memory management system (inspired by ownership and borrowing) that is efficient and safe.[20]

Powerful metaprogramming capabilities for generating specialized code.[21]

Leveraging MLIR for hardware-aware optimization.

Strategic Python interoperability for gradual performance improvements.[22]

It's important to note that Mojo is still under active development, and its full performance potential will continue to be realized as the language and its tooling mature. However, the design principles clearly prioritize high performance as a core feature.

As you delve deeper into Mojo, you'll likely encounter specific language features and libraries that further unlock its performance capabilities. Keep an eye on the official documentation and examples from Modular for the latest advancements in this area.

10.2 Introduction to Advanced Topics: Concurrency and More

Alright, buckle up! Now that we've laid a solid foundation with the fundamentals of Mojo, it's time to peek into some more advanced and powerful concepts that will allow you to build sophisticated and high-performance applications. Two key areas we'll touch upon are **concurrency** and a glimpse at other advanced topics you might encounter as you deepen your Mojo skills.

1. Concurrency:

Concurrency is the ability of a program to work on multiple tasks *at the same time* or *appear* to be doing so. It's a crucial concept for building responsive and efficient applications, especially in today's multi-core processor world.

Why Concurrency?

Responsiveness: In user interfaces, concurrency allows the application to remain responsive to user input even while performing long-running tasks in the background.

Performance: By dividing work into smaller, independent tasks that can run in parallel on multiple CPU cores, concurrency can significantly improve the overall performance of your application.

Handling Multiple Inputs: Servers and network applications often need to handle multiple incoming requests concurrently.

Common Concurrency Models:

Threads: Threads are lightweight units of execution within a process. Multiple threads can run concurrently and share the same memory space. However, managing shared memory between threads can be complex and prone to issues like race conditions and deadlocks.

Asynchronous Programming (Async/Await): This model allows you to write code that can perform long-running operations without blocking the main thread. Instead, the operation is started, and the program can continue with other tasks. When the operation completes, a callback or a continuation is executed. `async` and `await` keywords (common in many modern languages) often simplify asynchronous programming.

Actors: The actor model is a higher-level concurrency model where independent "actors" communicate with each other by sending messages. Each actor has its own state and processes messages sequentially, which can help avoid some of the complexities of shared-memory concurrency.

Concurrency in Mojo (Anticipated):
Given Mojo's focus on performance and its aim to be a systems programming language, it will likely provide robust support for concurrency. This might include:

Efficient threading primitives: Perhaps with built-in mechanisms to manage threads and synchronization safely.

A strong asynchronous programming model: Possibly using `async` and `await` keywords to make asynchronous code easier to write and reason about.

Potentially support for actor-based concurrency or other high-level concurrency abstractions.

Integration with hardware-level parallelism (e.g., SIMD, GPU computing) for even greater performance in concurrent tasks.

2. Other Advanced Topics:

Beyond concurrency, as you become more proficient in Mojo, you'll likely encounter other advanced topics that allow you to build more powerful and sophisticated applications:

Memory Management in Detail: While we touched on ownership and borrowing, a deeper understanding of Mojo's memory management model will be crucial for writing efficient and safe code, especially when interacting with lower-level systems or dealing with performance-critical applications.

Generics (Parametric Polymorphism): Generics allow you to write code that can work with different data types without sacrificing type safety. For example, you could write a single `List` class that can hold integers, strings, or any other type.

Traits/Interfaces: Traits (or interfaces in some languages) define a set of methods that a type must implement. They allow for polymorphism and code reuse by defining contracts between different types.

Error Handling (Beyond Basic `try`/`except`): More advanced error handling patterns, such as using `Result` types to explicitly represent the possibility of failure and propagate errors in a structured way.

Metaprogramming (Advanced): Deeper dives into Mojo's metaprogramming capabilities, including writing macros or using reflection to inspect and modify code at compile time or runtime.

Foreign Function Interface (FFI): The ability to interact with code written in other languages (like C or C++). This is important for leveraging existing libraries and for tasks that require direct access to system-level APIs.

Testing and Debugging (Advanced Techniques): More sophisticated testing strategies, profiling tools for identifying performance bottlenecks, and advanced debugging techniques for complex concurrent or asynchronous code.

Building Libraries and Frameworks: Understanding how to structure larger projects into reusable libraries and potentially contributing to or using application frameworks built in Mojo.

Domain-Specific Advanced Topics: Depending on your area of interest, you might delve into advanced topics related to machine learning (given Mojo's focus in this area), high-performance computing, or web development within the Mojo ecosystem.

The Journey Ahead:

Mastering these advanced topics will take time and practice. As Mojo continues to evolve, more resources and documentation will become available to guide you. The key is to build a strong foundation in the fundamentals first and then gradually explore these more intricate and powerful aspects of the language.

Which of these advanced topics pique your interest the most right now? Or is there anything specific within concurrency that you'd like to explore further conceptually?

10.3 Resources for Continued Learning and Growth in the Mojo Ecosystem

It's fantastic that you're thinking about your continued learning journey in the Mojo ecosystem! As Mojo is a relatively new language that is still under active development, the landscape of resources is continuously evolving. Here's a breakdown of where you can find valuable information and stay up-to-date:

1. Official Documentation and Resources from Modular:

Mojo Language Basics: The official Modular website provides introductory guides and documentation on the fundamentals of the Mojo language.[1] This is the most reliable source for accurate syntax and core concepts.

Check the Modular Mojo documentation pages.

Mojo Manual: Look for a comprehensive language manual that delves into various aspects of Mojo programming, from basic syntax to more advanced features.[2]

Mojo SDK Documentation: As you start building more complex applications, the SDK documentation will be crucial for understanding available libraries and tools.

Modular Blog: Keep an eye on the Modular blog for announcements, tutorials, and insights into the latest developments in Mojo.

https://www.modular.com/blog

GitHub Repository: The official Mojo GitHub repository (https://github.com/modular/mojo) is a great place to see the source code for examples, the standard library, and potentially contribute to the project as it matures. You can also track ongoing development and discussions.

2. Community Resources:

Discord Server: The Mojo community on Discord is a fantastic place to ask questions, share your progress, and connect with other Mojo enthusiasts and developers.[3] Look for an official invite link on the Modular website or GitHub repository.

Community Forums: Modular might host its own community forums where users can discuss Mojo-related topics in a more structured way than a chat platform. Check the official website for links.

Social Media: Follow Modular and key individuals in the Mojo team on platforms like Twitter/X and LinkedIn for announcements and insights.

3. Tutorials and Examples:

"Mojo By Example": This resource (https://ruhati.net/) offers a comprehensive introduction to Mojo with practical examples covering various language features.

GitHub Examples: The `examples` directory in the official Mojo GitHub repository contains a wealth of code snippets demonstrating different aspects of the language and its capabilities.[4]

Blog Posts and Articles: As the Mojo ecosystem grows, more independent blog posts and articles will emerge, offering tutorials and insights. Search for "Mojo programming tutorial" or similar terms.

Interactive Notebooks: Modular often provides interactive Jupyter notebooks that allow you to run Mojo code directly in your browser, making it easy to experiment and learn.[5] Look for these on their website or in the GitHub repository.

4. Books and Courses:

While Mojo is still new, keep an eye out for books specifically dedicated to learning the language. Some introductory books are already available.

Online learning platforms like Coursera, Udemy, and others might eventually host courses on Mojo.

Tips for Continued Learning:

Start with the official documentation: This will give you the most accurate and up-to-date information.

Experiment with the code: The best way to learn is by doing. Try modifying examples and writing your own small programs.

Engage with the community: Ask questions and share your learnings on the Discord server or forums.

Follow the development: Stay informed about the latest features and changes by following the official blog and GitHub repository.

Be patient: As a young language, the ecosystem is still evolving. New resources will continue to emerge over time.

By actively engaging with these resources, you'll be well-equipped to continue your learning journey and grow with the Mojo ecosystem!

www.ingramcontent.com/pod-product-compliance
Lightning Source LLC
LaVergne TN
LVHW051735050326
832903LV00023B/933